D1590109

THE INTELLIGENT EAR

On the Nature of Sound Perception

THE INTELLIGENT EAR

On the Nature of Sound Perception

Reinier Plomp
Professor Emeritus
Free University Amsterdam

LEA

LAWRENCE ERLBAUM ASSOCIATES, PUBLISHERS
2002   Mahwah, New Jersey   London

612.3 9
P 729

Lawrence Erlbaum Associates, Inc., Publishers
10 Industrial Avenue
Mahwah, NJ 07430

Cover design by Kathryn Houghtaling Lacey

Library of Congress Cataloging-in-Publication Data

Plomp, Reinier.
The intelligent ear : on the nature of sound perception
Reinier Plomp.
p. cm.
Includes bibliographical references and index.
ISBN 0-8058-3867-8 (alk. paper)
1. Auditory perception. I. Title.
QP465 .P564   2001
612.8'5—dc21   2001023646
                                                          CIP

Printed in the United States of America
10 9 8 7 6 5 4 3 2 1

Contents

Preface

Twenty-five years ago, I published a monograph entitled *Aspects of Tone Sensation*, dealing with the psychophysics of simple and complex tones. Since that time, auditory perception as a field of study has undergone a radical metamorphosis. Technical and methodological innovations, as well as a considerable increase in attention to the various aspects of our auditory experience, have changed the picture profoundly.

This book is an attempt to account for this development, not by considering the new attainments one by one, but by giving a comprehensive survey of the present state of the art as a whole. My point of departure is the auditory reality we deal with in everyday life, the fact that we are continuously confronted with many simultaneous sound streams such as those produced by motor cars, musical instruments, and, most important, human speakers. Traditionally, hearing has been studied in a rather abstract way, considered in terms of parameters manipulated under "clean" laboratory conditions rather than as accomplished under the confounded conditions of the world outside. Moreover, the auditory and cognitive aspects of listening to complex sounds have mostly been studied more or less independently as two successive stages of auditory processing, rather than as different facets of the same process. I have attempted to break with this tradition by focusing on the superposition of complex sound streams rather than the abstractions of single sound "units"—tone pulses or speech phonemes—as a means of judging whether our descriptions and theories are valid. It is for the reader to decide whether this approach has been successful or not.

This preference for an inclusive approach explains the book's title. Nowadays it is fashionable to speak about "intelligent" computers and machines, so it may be time to also speak of the "intelligent" ear, as R. L. Gregory did for the eye in 1970, more than 30 years ago. To do this, I have restricted myself to what I consider to be the basic characteristics of the hearing process. There are many books dealing with topics such as hearing thresholds for tones, just-noticeable differences in frequency and amplitude, the ear's sensitivity to differences in

speech sounds, and so on, so I have not referred to any such established knowledge that is not directly related to the theme of the book.

The ideas presented in this book could not have been generated without the
continuous interactions I have enjoyed with my colleagues and coworkers at
the Institute for Perception TNO at Soesterberg and the Free University at Amsterdam. In particular, I would like to mention Tammo Houtgast, Louis Pols,
Pim Levelt, Guido Smoorenburg, and Joost Festen as having stimulated my
thinking profoundly over the years. Although I am solely responsible for the
contents of the book, I am very grateful for their cooperation during more than
40 years of auditory research in the Netherlands.

In a quite different way, I owe much to the numerous foreign colleagues I became acquainted with, particularly in America. Since I entered the field of audition in 1953 as an acoustically oriented physicist, the most profound influences
on my experimental work as well as my scientific thinking (apart from
Helmholtz, the great German inspirer) have been their papers published in the
Journal of the Acoustical Society of America. My first journey to America in 1966
brought me into personal contact with many colleagues at the fall meeting of
the Acoustical Society of America, with visits to a large number of laboratories
all over the United States. Since that year, close relations have been maintained
between us over the years.

During one of these visits, Ira Hirsh introduced me to his former coworker
Judy Lauter, who, in addition to her fascination with speech perception, was
also extremely interested in the paintings of Rembrandt, even to the extent of
writing poems about them. Her visits to the Netherlands brought me into closer
contact with her, and after having finished the manuscript, I considered it a
privilege to find that she was willing to serve as a critical editor of this book. Her
expert knowledge and experience, both in linguistics and speech perception research, have greatly improved the text, not only with respect to linguistic irreg-
ularities but also for conceptual clarification in difficult passages. I am
extremely grateful for her contribution. Of course, I am the only one to blame
for less appropriate expressions that may remain due to my persistence.

Finally, I would like to thank Emily Wilkinson, who, many years ago as an editor at Academic Press, London, stimulated me to write *Aspects of Tone Sensation*, and more recently, in the same function at Lawrence Erlbaum Associates,
has encouraged me to write the present book. In both cases, contacts with her
have been extremely helpful and stimulating.

                                                           — *Reinier Plomp*

1
Introduction

The aim of hearing research is to obtain a better understanding of how sounds presented to the ear are translated by the hearing process into sounds as percepts. In agreement with common usage, the word *sound* is used here ambiguously in two different meanings: in a physical sense as air vibrations originating from a source, and in a perceptual sense referring to how these vibrations are heard.

It may seem that using the same term for both cause and effect is confusing. If the context of the word does not give adequate information, this is true. Generally, however, the use of a single word has its significance. In everyday life, we are usually surrounded by many sound sources. When we say that we hear one or another "sound" we refer to our ability to identify the various percepts one to one with their sources. Implicitly, such usage also indicates that although the vibrations produced by the various sound sources are superimposed seemingly inextricably in the air, the ear is able to disentangle these vibrations so faithfully that we are not aware of the fact that they were ever mixed.

This amazing achievement demonstrates how well our hearing is matched to its task: to present us with a reliable representation of the world of sound sources around us. As the following chapters show, this is a far from easy task. It requires special processes to seek out which sound components belong together and to capture each individual sound with its associated characteristics. These processes cannot be considered as exclusively passive. They are so sophisticated that they have to be seen as active processes. They operate so perfectly, interpreting every new sound against the background of earlier experiences, that it is fully justified to qualify them as *intelligent* processes.

Before starting a more detailed discussion of the perception of sound, attention to some general aspects of hearing is given in this chapter. Our present knowledge is the cumulative product of a historical development of more than a century. For an appropriate evaluation of the state of the art, it is worthwhile to trace the forces that have dominated its past.

The course of science has many curves, detours, and dead ends. At the outset, they may all present themselves as well-paved roads, each quite suitable for reaching a scientific goal in a highly efficient way. Hearing research has not been free of such temptations. In order to see them in the right perspective and to realize their almost universal character as manifestations of the *Zeitgeist*, some of these tempting detours are discussed here in more general terms. This helps us in the following chapters to recognize the role these different approaches have played in hearing research and to understand the impact they have had. Although they are not mutually independent, I distinguish four types of scientific preferences or biases that have affected the history of hearing research: (a) the dominance of sinusoidal tones as stimuli, (b) the predilection for a "microscopic" (as opposed to a macroscopic) approach, (c) emphasis on the psychophysical (rather than the cognitive) aspects of hearing, and (d) focus on stimuli abstracted from the "dirty" acoustical conditions of everyday listening.

THE DOMINANCE OF SINUSOIDAL TONES

The impressive successes of physics in the 19th century had, without doubt, quite stimulating effects on the beginnings of psychophysics. Moreover, this new branch of science took as its task the study of the relations between the outer physical world and its inner, perceptual, counterpart. As the percepts appear to mirror the physical world so strikingly, it seemed natural that they should be described as obeying similar laws. Moreover, the first knowledge of the eye and the ear concerned the peripheral organs, for which physical principles are indeed extremely important.

In the course of the 19th century, Fourier's theorem, stating that any periodical function with period duration T can be described as the sum of sinusoidal functions with period durations T/n ($n = 1, 2, 3, \ldots$), was enthusiastically applied by physicists in their studies of mechanical vibrations. It is little wonder that the theorem also became a keystone of modern hearing theory. The attention of students of hearing became more and more narrowly focused on considering how sinusoidal tones, those denoted as *pure* tones, are perceived.

A striking illustration is *Hearing—Its Psychology and Physiology*, published in 1938 by Stanley Smith Stevens (1906–1973) and Hallowell Davis (1896–1992), the most important book on audition for many years and rightly appreciated as a classic in its field. In this book, attention was almost exclusively focused on how single pure tones are perceived and how they interact in the form of beats and combination tones. The fact that the tones we hear every day are *not* sinusoidal was scarcely considered, with the consequence that even such basic aspects as pitch and timbre received a rather unsatisfactory treatment.

This primary interest in sinusoidal sounds dominated hearing research up to the 1960s. Of course, this period should not be seen as only negative. It represented an essential and important stage in the progress of our knowledge, yielding valuable information on the frequency-resolving power of the ear and the selective transfer of this information by the auditory nerve to higher centers in the brain. However, in that abstract sinusoidal tone pulses are remote from the everyday sounds of speech and music, their overestimation as perceptual elements delayed fresh insights regarding the perception of more "real" sounds.

Since the 1960s, this picture has changed in two ways. In the first place, the role of harmonics in the perception of tones has received much more attention. The most important result of this change has been a rethinking of the way in which pitch is derived from the stimulus. Second, the study of single tones has been extended to series of *successive* tones, an extension that has led to quite surprising results. They are discussed in the next two chapters.

These developments marked a fundamental turning point in our views on hearing. In the old view, the ear's frequency-resolution mechanism could be compared quite satisfactorily with a series of band filters, and hearing was seen as a *passive* process. More recent experimental evidence has revealed, however, that the auditory system cannot be explained any longer in terms of passive processes only, but that *active* processes, too, are involved. These rather recent modifications of our insights indicate that the processes required for framing a faithful perceptual picture of the world of sounds reaching the ears are much more sophisticated than previously thought.

THE PREDILECTION FOR
A "MICROSCOPIC" APPROACH

The preference for studying sinusoidal tones is not just an accidental phenomenon but may be seen as the concrete application of a scientific ideal. The remarkable successes of physics since the 17th century have had a great impact on ideas of how nature in general should be studied. They strongly suggested that the best way to find relations between causes and consequences in complex systems is to concentrate on manageable small subsystems. Take as an example the problem of calculating the speed of free-falling objects. The physicist selects a heavy object, carefully shaped to minimize the effect of air resistance; furthermore, he or she eliminates as much as possible other potentially disturbing factors, such as temperature fluctuations, air movements, and so on. The physicist may select as the only independent variable the distance to a surface hit by the object, and ensure that the object is made to fall exactly the same way on every trial. Then, by measuring the time required to reach the surface as a function of distance, the experimenter determines how the speed of a free-falling body increases with time.

Such an experimental setup is characterized by the following ideal program: (a) isolate a small subsystem from the physical world, (b) eliminate all "disturbing" factors, (c) hold all parameters constant except one, and then (d) investigate the effect of varying that single parameter.

It was very tempting to apply this same approach to the study of perception. A good example is the study of auditory sensitivity as a function of frequency. The experimenter (a) selects a sinusoidal tone as the most elementary auditory stimulus (the "isolated small subsystem"), (b) eliminates "disturbing" factors such as signal distortion and ambient or equipment noise, (c) holds tone duration, experimental procedure, and so on constant, and then (d) determines the sound-pressure level required to reach a listener's perceptual threshold as a function of tone frequency.

Experiments carried out according to this scheme have taught us much about the way such sounds are perceived. Of course, the reduction of the world of dynamic sounds to such simple subsystems meant that scientists were actually studying abstractions of everyday perception, but this was not seen as a disadvantage. On the contrary, "divide and rule" was the powerful motto of this approach, which is still accepted by many investigators as the most appropriate way to study how the complex acoustic reality is perceived.

There are, however, strong arguments that such reasoning is not as watertight as it may at first seem to be—not only in studies of perception but also in physics, where the approach has enjoyed such success. The problem is that this reasoning presupposes tacitly that once the behavior of all subsystems is described, no further data will be needed to account for the behavior of the system as a whole. This seemingly self-evident point of view is simply not correct.

The insufficiency of the elementary subsystems approach can be demonstrated by a basic example given by the German physicist Max Planck (1858–1947) in a series of lectures on theoretical physics presented in 1909 at Columbia University in New York (Planck, 1915/1998). In these lectures, he explained the fundamental difference between the First and Second Laws of thermodynamics by considering a hypothetical *microscopic* and a *macroscopic* observer.

In order to study the dynamics of gas molecules, the microscopic observer chooses to isolate a single molecule as a subsystem and to follow its movements.

This investigator finds that these movements obey the law of conservation of energy, known as the First Law of thermodynamics. The macroscopic observer, on the other hand, focuses attention on an ensemble of molecules behaving as a whole. This investigator discovers that this ensemble maximizes entropy (complete disorder), illustrating the Second Law of thermodynamics.

Planck's point was that the microscopic observer will never discover the Second Law because it is a *statistical* law relating to a large ensemble, not applicable to the single molecule. The example demonstrates that, even in basic physics, investigations that focus exclusively on subsystems may fall short of explaining fully the system as a whole. The microscopic approach needs a macroscopic supplement for a full understanding of nature. It is notable that Planck concluded: "It appears to me as though a similar difficulty presents itself in most of the problems of intellectual life." (p. 98)

Indeed, if macroscopic as well as microscopic observers are needed in physics, we can be sure that, a fortiori, it holds all the more for the highly complex phenomenon involved in perception. Gardner (1985) used almost the same terms as Planck in distinguishing between "*molecular* or small-scale units of analysis and *molar* or large-scale units of analysis":

> Some programs, such as those of traditional psychophysics and contemporary information processing, show a penchant for small-scale units (bits, individual percepts, single associations examined in brief periods of time) on the assumption that a thorough understanding of these elementary units and processes is the surest path toward the ultimate explanation of complex units and entities. A contrasting faith is found among proponents of the molar approach—those who look at large-scale problems tackled over a long period of time and invoke analytic concepts like schemas, frames, or strategies.... One can embrace a molecular (or a molar) approach for different reasons: some psychologists begin with a molecular approach in the hope of being able to adapt their methods to molar entities; while others believe that ultimately all behavior can be reduced to, and explained by, molecular entities. (pp. 96–97)

In reviewing the history of psychology, Gardner pointed out that great 19th-century scientists such as Hermann von Helmholtz (1821–1894) and Wilhelm Wundt (1832–1920) were quite aware of the need for employing both approaches. He described the "behaviorist revolution" as exclusively favoring the molecular approach, abandoning gestalt psychology's molar attention to the whole as an out-of-date holdover from a past century.

Gardner's classification of traditional psychophysics and information processing as molecular approaches was quite correct. The microscopic observers dominated sensory psychology. They were convinced they could complete the house of perception by laying elementary-subsystem bricks one by one.

In the case of sound perception, this means that there was a common belief that studying sounds at an elementary level—isolated "pure" tones in psychophysics and phonemes in speech research—would yield a reliable picture of how everyday sounds are perceived. As a consequence, attention was so exclusively directed to such elements that important global phenomena remained unexamined. In spite of this, model makers were inclined to extend their limited knowledge to topics considerably exceeding their data. As the following chapters show, many conclusions based on studies with elementary stimuli have appeared to be wrong in the light of later research utilizing a more molar approach. We will find ample evidence of this fact. It will become clear that the macroscopic point of view is essential and at least as important as the microscopic approach for explaining the perception of the complex sounds of everyday life.

THE PREFERENCE FOR THE PSYCHOPHYSICAL ASPECTS OF PERCEPTION

The examples just presented may have given the impression that hearing is entirely, or almost entirely, determined by auditory processes in which stimuli are translated simply into sensations. However, this is not the case. The perception process yields not only the *sensation* of an incoming stimulus, but also its (unconscious) *interpretation* in the context of previous experience. Without the latter aspect, our perceptual abilities would be limited to those of a young infant with restricted auditory experience.

That is, hearing includes both audition and cognition. I will use *audition* to refer to the activities of what is traditionally considered as the hearing organ proper, whereas *cognition* will refer to the interpretation of the output of these activities. The difference between audition and cognition has also been expressed in the terms *bottom-up* and *top-down* processing. Audition can be primarily seen as bottom-up processing stressing the significance of information in the actual stimulus, versus cognition as top-down processing stressing the significance of concepts, expectations, and memory as a context for stimulus perception.

To some extent, this distinction is different from the one contrasting the microscopic and macroscopic points of view. Loudness, pitch, and timbre as qualities of nonsinusoidal sounds are definitely macroscopic in nature, but it would be confusing to consider them as cognitive attributes or as the results of top-down processing. Nevertheless, there is a close relation—the microscopic approach usually focuses on bottom-up processing, whereas the macroscopic approach typically considers top-down factors as well. As Gardner (1985) expressed it:

The contrast between molecular and molar approaches resembles, but is by no means identical to the distinction between the *top-down* and the *bottom-up* approaches. In a top-down approach, which has rationalist overtones, the subject is assumed to bring to the task his own schemes, strategies, or frames which strongly color his performance. In a bottom-up approach, more allied to the empiricist camp, the actual details of a focal task or situation are assumed to exert primary influence on a subject's performance. (p. 97)

The important role of cognition appears most clearly in the perception of speech. It manifests itself in the difference between listening to speech in an unfamiliar foreign language versus one's native language. The auditory aspects in both cases may be comparable, but the perceptual outcome is entirely different, and the difference represents the contribution of top-down processing based on knowledge of the language. This knowledge includes a large mental vocabulary, familiarity with the linguistics of sentences and the semantic importance of voice intonation, the ability to distinguish between relevant and irrelevant variations in pronunciation, and so on. All these factors determine whether a speech signal will be heard as meaningful or not.

Because the scientific strategies for studying audition and cognition are so different, there is a constant danger that these two aspects of hearing are studied independently. Auditory perception can be studied psychophysically without any consideration of a possible role of cognitive factors (although "subject variables" are often defined in these experiments). Particularly in the study of speech perception, this can result in conclusions that are not justified. As chapters 4 and 5 show, the significance of cognition in the perception of elementary speech sounds is so different from its significance in the perception of fluent speech that we have to be very careful in extrapolating seemingly obvious conclusions based on the study of phonemes to apply to the perception of sentences.

In addition, audition and cognition should not be understood as different stages of hearing—that is, that bottom-up processing leads to a sensation and, subsequently, top-down processing is employed to interpret this sensation. In fact, the situation is much more complex, with both processes working in parallel. We will see that the *same* sound may be perceived rather differently, depending on the listener's unconscious or conscious extrapolations. What we hear depends on what we expect to hear.

ABSTRACTIONS FROM "DIRTY" EVERYDAY CONDITIONS

Finally, certain constraints of the "culture" of studying sound perception should not be overlooked. Although as a person the experimenter is daily exposed to a complex world of sounds, as a scientist he or she is trained to tolerate only "clean" stimuli in the laboratory. This choice necessarily distorts estimates of the achievements of the hearing system, and also affects the ways in which experimental results may be conceptualized. The laboratory situation narrows the experimenter's view.

Perhaps nowhere else has the deficiency of this approach been expressed more directly than in the field of memory research. In his book *Memory in the Real World*, Cohen (1989) referred to the opening paper presented by U. Neisser during a conference in 1976 as a milestone in the psychology of memory. It is indeed revealing to quote from this paper with its significant title: "Memory: What Are the Important Questions?" (Neisser, 1978):

> I am often unable to recall the authors of phrases that I would like to quote, and have equal difficulty in remembering who told me things. These retrieval failures pose some interesting questions. Why do they occur? Do other people have less trouble recalling sources than I do? Is my difficulty in remembering the source of a written quotation related to other types of memory failure, or are they independent? In fact, how does one go about remembering sources, or arguments, or material appropriate to one's train of thought? What makes for skill in such activities?
>
> These questions may not be the "important" ones that my title has promised, but they are interesting nevertheless. They involve real uses of memory in humanly understandable situations. It is therefore discouraging to find that nothing in the extensive literature of the psychology of memory sheds much light on them, so that anyone who wishes to study such problems must start from scratch. Unfortunately, this is not an isolated instance. It is an example of a principle that is nearly as valid in 1978 as it was in 1878: If X is an interesting or socially significant aspect of memory, then psychologists have hardly ever studied X. (pp. 3–4)

But Neisser also recognized that the desire for well-controlled laboratory conditions was part of the explanation:

> The psychologists who have spent a century studying esoteric forms of memory in the laboratory are not really uninterested in its more ordinary manifestations, and have always hoped that their work would have wide applicability sooner or later. Their preference for artificial tasks has a rational basis: one can control variables and manipulate conditions more easily in the lab than in natural settings. Why not work under the best possible conditions? Memory is memory, or so it would seem.... Unfortunately, it turned out that "learning" in general does not exist: wasps and songbirds and rats integrate past experiences into their lives in very different ways. I think that "memory" in general does not exist either. (p. 13)

I resist the temptation to quote more fascinating passages, and close with the end of the article:

> The realistic study of memory is much harder than the work we have been accustomed to: so much harder that one can easily forgive those who have been reluctant to under-

take it. After all, we bear no malice toward that legendary drunk who kept looking for his money under the streetlamp although he had dropped it ten yards away in the dark. As he correctly pointed out, the light was better where he was looking. But what we want to find *is* in the dark, out there where real people make use of their pasts in complicated ways. If we are to find it, we must look there. (pp. 19–20)

It is not difficult to recognize this same problem[1] in hearing research. Many investigators have assumed that full knowledge of how sinusoidal tones are heard will be sufficient to explain the perception of everyday sounds. A long time ago, a well-known Dutch composer visited me, presuming that current laboratory knowledge of tone perception could help him to a better understanding of how musical sounds are perceived. I had to disappoint him.

Without doubt, the largest discrepancy between the listening conditions in the laboratory versus the acoustic reality of the outside world is manifest in the exclusion of noise in the first case, contrasted with the presence of a complex of usually strong and disruptive sounds in the latter. In the laboratory, the experimenter tries to create stimuli that are as "clean" as possible, free from interfering noises, which leads to a strong bias for avoiding experimental conditions in which unrelated sounds interact. As a result, everyday auditory experience is essentially eliminated from the field of study.

DISCUSSION

The explanation presented will have made clear that the field of sound perception is a far from boring landscape. It has been, and still is, an interdisciplinary intellectual arena controlled by quite divergent forces. Many investigators remain loyal adherents of the microscopic approach, whether or not they use complex stimuli, whereas others, still in the minority, prefer to be considered as macroscopic observers. At the same time, many researchers are interested in the auditory aspects and others, again a minority, in the cognitive aspects, of hearing. This may not be surprising, as the study of hearing is a meeting point of several disciplines—such biases can be partly explained by the different backgrounds that scientists bring to their tasks. To use two extremes as an example: physicists will be more predisposed toward the microscopic study of audition, and linguists will favor the macroscopic study of cognition.

Looking back over the last half century, we may discern a trend. For all of the four preferences or biases listed, there has been a definite shift in the direc-

---

[1]For a discussion of the role of reality in studying memory, see the articles introduced by Loftus (1991).

tion of studies involving more complex stimuli and more concern with the macroscopic (holistic) and the cognitive aspects of sound perception. This trend may be least clear for the fourth point, accepting everyday conditions as the ultimate criteria for framing perceptual rules, which has still not received the attention it deserves.

Without doubt, the mutual understanding of scientists using the various approaches has increased considerably in these 50 years. Nevertheless, there are still many investigators who are so involved in their own research that they seem not to be interested in the results of studies representing other, equally respectable, points of view. We will encounter several such cases in the course of the following chapters. These blind spots can be explained in part by the huge increase in the literature on auditory perception over this period. Whereas half a century ago it was not difficult to follow new developments over the entire field of sound perception, this has become practically impossible in more recent years.

There are no recipes for avoiding scientific provincialism. Personally, I believe that the most relevant criterion for evaluating one's own work on auditory perception is to ask whether it contributes to a better insight into the perception of everyday sounds. In 1953, Wolfgang Metzger (1899–1979)[2] published his classic *Gesetze des Sehens* (*Laws of Vision*). In this book, Metzger, a pupil of Wolfgang Köhler (1887–1967) and Max Wertheimer (1880–1943), devoted only a single, but in my view highly important, paragraph to the subject of hearing. Since the time I discovered this passage almost half a century ago, I have read it again and again, because it contains a message I have never found so clearly pronounced in any text on hearing. Abridged in English, it reads:

> The achievements of the ear are indeed fabulous. While I am writing, my elder son rattles the fire rake in the stove, the infant babbles contentedly in his baby carriage, the church clock strikes the hour, a car stops in front of the house, next door one of the girls is practicing on the piano, at the front door her mother converses with a messenger, and I can also hear the fine scraping of the point of the pencil and my hand moving on the paper. In the vibrations of air striking my ear, all these sounds are superimposed into a single extremely complex stream of pressure waves. Without doubt the achievements of the ear are greater than those of the eye. Why do the psychologists, particularly the Germans, stick so stubbornly to *vision* research? (pp. 59–60)

We should never forget that these observations represent the true nature of hearing. They tell us that in everyday listening we are *not* confronted with a single undisturbed sound but by an acoustic complex from multiple sources, from which we have to extract the one sound in which we are interested. If this is the

---

[2]For a short biography, see Ash (1995).

"normal" condition of auditory perception, it should surely be a *major* criterion for evaluating any model of perception. Our research should be ultimately directed to elucidating the complex processes underlying our achievements in everyday hearing. Indeed, such achievements can only be accomplished by an "intelligent ear."

CONCLUSIONS

The remarkable ability of our hearing system to translate the complex acoustic world around us into a comprehensible perceptual image requires the close cooperation of *auditory* processing of a more passive type and *cognitive* processing of a more active type. In order to obtain an accurate picture of these achievements, studies on how elementary sounds are perceived must be complemented by studies on how ensembles of sounds are perceived. This is true for the perception of tones but is particularly crucial for the perception of speech, where intelligibility depends so strongly on past experience.

2
The Perception of Single Sounds

We are all aware that, just as we can distinguish different visual objects, the hearing system is able to distinguish different sounds. This holds not only for "single" sounds such as the successive tones of a melody or the successive vowels and consonants of a word, but even for simultaneous sounds such as those produced by multiple musical instruments in a concert or the mix of voices at a cocktail party. Perhaps the most striking property of the hearing system is its ability to *analyze* the world of superimposed sounds and to separate them according to their various sources.

However, as will become clear, this is only one part of the story. Each individual sound consists of several frequency components. The ear distinguishes between frequency components originating from different sound sources, as opposed to components from the same source. It separates out components according to the first category, but not the second. This calls for an extremely sophisticated process, exceeding by far the performance of any frequency analyzer designed for acoustical research, in that auditory perception involves *synthesis* as well as analysis. The analyzing process "overshoots" its task of separating the individual sounds, and then a subsequent synthesizing process is employed to "repair" the defects, resulting in an astonishingly reliable picture of the world of sounds reaching the ear.

This combination of processes—both passive (analysis of components) and active (grouping by source)—is discussed in this and the next chapter. This chapter deals with the frequency-analyzing power of the ear, as well as with how sounds are characterized perceptually in terms of timbre, pitch, and loudness. Even single sounds require synthesis as a necessary complement of analysis. In the next chapter, this treatment is extended to the case of multiple simultaneous sounds. Additional sophisticated processes appear to be needed to ensure that the components of different simultaneous sound streams are sorted appropriately and that these streams are perceived as if they have never been mixed.

THE EAR AS A FREQUENCY ANALYZER

Any tone, whether produced by a musical instrument or by the vibrating human larynx, can be described physically as a periodic variation of air pressure. The duration of each period of vibration determines the pitch of the sound, whereas waveform characteristics determine its timbre. The ear is able to process sounds in such a way that both pitch and timbre of each individual sound are traced. This implies that the ear separates, in one way or another, these sounds in terms of their period duration as well as their waveform. This may seem an easy task, but it in fact requires a very ingenious analyzer.

Actually, the problem is "solved" in a two-stage process, a straightforward analysis followed by partial synthesis to counteract the effects of the too-rigorous first stage. This processing is so complex that it can be very difficult to simulate its performance. The first analyzing stage is one that is well known in engineering. It is realized in the cochlea by means of a hydromechanical system that analyzes the incoming sound into sinusoidal components. Of course, just as with electronic frequency analyzers, this system has its limits, which can be described in terms of the so-called masked threshold (50% chance of hearing) of a second sinusoidal tone presented simultaneously with the sinusoidal stimulus.

For actual measurements, in order to avoid unwanted interferences between two sinusoids, the stimulus is typically replaced with a narrow band of noise with randomly changing phase, which has a definite tonal quality. As an example, Fig. 2.1 shows the masked thresholds of narrow bands of noise centered at 250, 1,000, and 4,000 Hz. We see that the curves have very steep slopes, indicating that the ear can readily separate simultaneous tonal components that differ in frequency by more than, say, 50%.

Such masking curves are often compared to electric band filters specified by bandwidth, that is, the width of their peaks. For the ear, this bandwidth, known as the *critical bandwidth*, is between $^1/_4$ and $^1/_3$ octave, roughly about 20% of each band's center frequency. Figure 2.2 represents the critical bandwidth as the best estimate based on a large number of different measurement approaches. Note that, over the entire frequency range, the critical bandwidth is (approximately) the same percentage, *not* the same absolute frequency difference. This is related to the property of the ear of "counting" in frequency ratios rather than in absolute frequencies, also reflected in the musical scale with its octaves (1:2), fifths (2:3), fourths (3:4), and so on. However, it is important to note that the use of

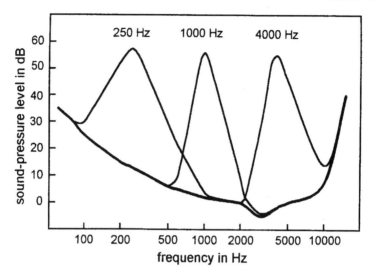

FIG. 2.1. Masked threshold of narrow bands of noise centered at 250 Hz, 1000 Hz, and 4000 Hz. The lower curve represents the absolute hearing threshold.

the terms *band filter* and *bandwidth* should not be understood as suggesting that the ear consists of a fixed series of band filters. This is definitely not the case. The ear's frequency-resolving power is essentially comparable to the eye's capacity to separate spatially different stimuli. The "filter" concept is only a way to describe the process in physical terms.

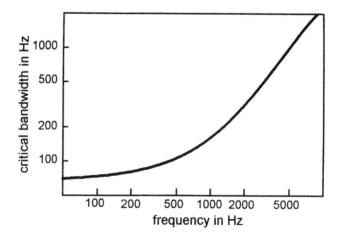

FIG. 2.2. Critical bandwidth as a function of frequency.

Let us now examine how this filtering system "overshoots" the task for which it is meant. Such a system would be an ideal analyzer if all sound sources produced only sinusoidal tones. In cases where multiple sources were producing tones, the system could split the superimposed vibrations faithfully into the components radiated from the various sound sources. The problem for the hearing system is, however, that the most common periodic sounds in the real world are *not* single sinusoids but a number of *combined* sinusoids. Figure 2.3 illustrates a periodic vibration composed of a series of six sinusoidal components of frequencies f, $2f$, $3f$, $4f$, $5f$, and $6f$ (the *harmonics*). The frequency of the lowest harmonic (the *fundamental*) is the primary determinant of the pitch of the tone, whereas the relative amplitudes of the different harmonics determine the timbre of the tone. In order to distinguish such a tone from a sinusoidal tone, it can be defined as a *complex* tone and the harmonics designated as *simple* tones.

The puzzle regarding the perception of complex tones is that we do not perceive such tones (as produced, e.g., by a musical instrument or the human

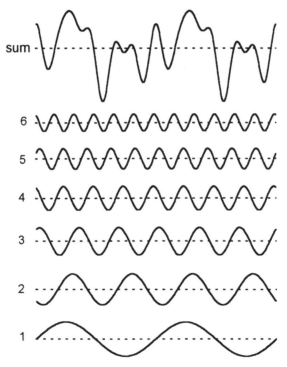

FIG. 2.3.   The upper periodic vibration is the sum of six sinusoidal vibrations with frequency ratios of 1:2:3:4:5:6.

voice) as a chord, but as a *single* tonal event, a unified percept with a characteristic pitch and timbre.

Thus the crucial question is: Are the individual harmonics actually inaudible? For the answer to this question, we go back in history.

Marin Mersenne (1588–1648) seems to have been the first scientist who observed that something interesting was going on in a vibrating string. In letters (de Waard, 1946) to Isaac Beeckman (1588–1637) and René Descartes (1596–1650), he asked whether they had an explanation for his observation that if one listens carefully to the sound, a number of different tones can be distinguished with pitches corresponding to 1, 2, 3, 4, and 5 times the pitch of the musical note. In his *Traité des Instrumens* (Mersenne, 1636), he described his observation as follows:

> The string struck and sounded freely makes at least five sounds at the same time, the first of which is the natural sound of the string and serves as the foundation for the rest.... [All these sounds] follow the ratio of the numbers 1, 2, 3, 4, 5, for one hears four sounds other than the natural one, the first of which is the octave above, the second is the twelfth, the third is the fifteenth, and the fourth is the major seventeenth. (p. 32)

Neither of his two correspondents mentioned was able to explain the phenomenon. Later on, it became more and more clear that the string of a violin vibrates not only over its entire length (thus generating the fundamental), but also in parts, producing multiple harmonics.

The mathematical proof that any periodic vibration can be described as the sum of sinusoidal vibrations with frequency ratios 1:2:3:4: ... was given by Joseph Fourier (1768–1830). After Helmholtz made Fourier's theorem the basis of his famous *Lehre von den Tonempfindungen als physiologische Grundlage für die Theorie der Musik* (von Helmholtz, 1863/1954), the concept of the ear as a Fourier-type frequency analyzer was universally accepted. Helmholtz was quite aware of the difficulties in hearing the partial tones of a vibrating string:

> Any one who endeaveours for the first time to distinguish the upper partial tones of a musical tone, generally finds considerable difficulty in merely hearing them.... I shall first give a description of such processes as will most easily put an untrained observer into a position to recognise upper partial tones, and I will remark in passing that a musically trained ear will not necessarily hear upper partial tones with greater ease and certainty than an untrained ear. (p. 49)

We do not follow Helmholtz here in his ingenious tricks to attempt to hear out the harmonics. Many years ago, I discovered that, surprisingly, no later investigator had ever tried to repeat his observations with modern methods to obtain a reliable estimate of the number of harmonics that can be distinguished under favorable conditions. It seemed to me that the best procedure was to present the listener with a complex tone consisting of a series of equally strong harmonics with frequencies f, $2f$, $3f$, $4f$, and so on, and also provide the listener with two sinusoidal tones, one with frequency nf, the other with frequency $(n \pm \frac{1}{2})f$, with $n = 1, 2, 3, 4, \ldots$ The listener could switch between the three tones, with the task to decide which sinusoidal tone was also present in the complex tone (Plomp & Mimpen, 1964). This procedure offers the listener the optimal means of directing attention to the harmonic component to be heard out. Because the score in this two-alternative forced-choice procedure can vary between 50% and 100%, 75% correct responses was accepted as the threshold criterion.

Figure 2.4 presents the mean threshold for six listeners (Plomp & Mimpen, 1968). The average number of five to six distinguishable harmonics agrees strikingly well with Mersenne's observations. As these figures indicate that only harmonics separated more than about 20% can be heard individually, the results provide additional evidence of the frequency distance earlier defined as the critical bandwidth. Moore and Ohgushi (1993) tested listeners with inharmonically related tone complexes, where all tones were equally separated in terms of critical bandwidth. They found that the audibility score of the individual components increased from 46% for their narrowest spacing of ¾ critical band to 90% for the widest spacing of 2 critical bands. We may conclude that the limit of listeners' ability to hear out the harmonics of a complex tone agrees rather well with the ear's frequency-resolving power.

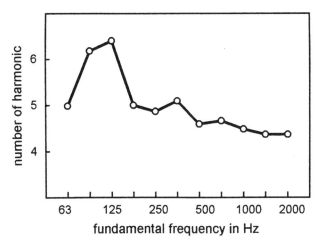

FIG. 2.4.   Average number (6 subjects) of individually distinguishable harmonics of a complex tone plotted as a function of the frequency of the fundamental (based on data from Plomp & Mimpen, 1968).

So it seems that the auditory system is a rather strange frequency analyzer indeed. We have found that, if listeners are queried in the right way, the perception of complex tones does obey the general rule—that is, listeners *can* hear out individual harmonics. However, the experience of listening to complex tones in everyday situations also indicates that the stage of frequency separation along the inner ear's basilar membrane is apparently followed by a process that annuls the first-stage analysis into separate harmonics. We might predict that this process makes use of the simple frequency ratios among the harmonics to yield an overall gestalt percept of the complex tone.

It is rather mysterious how the ear, on the one hand, can separate sinusoids originating from different sources, yet on the other, works to blend into a single percept the harmonics of the same tone. One can study this latter "fusion" process by synthesizing complex tones with harmonics deviating somewhat from their correct values. Informal listening tests indicate that as long as these deviations are less than, say, 0.5%, the harmonics remain fused. For larger deviations, the complex tone loses its unequivocal pitch and integrity and begins to sound more and more like a set of independent tones.

The unique phenomenon in which several sinusoidal tones with frequency ratios 1:2:3:4: … are normally perceived as a single tone has certainly played a decisive role in the selection and development of musical instruments. Given this rule of perception, it is not surprising that most instruments have strings or air columns as their vibrating matter, because such one-dimensional vibrational sources produce series of harmonically related vibrations (transversal in strings and longitudinal in air columns). In contrast, plates and membranes, with two-dimensional vibration patterns, are much less suited for producing sounds with a distinct pitch.

The requirement that a melodious musical instrument must be able to generate harmonically related partial tones can be illustrated nicely by the history of cast bells. Since the Middle Ages, many towers in the Low Countries have had carillons that were played regularly to announce the hours and entertain the people. By their nature, bells (which are more like plates than a column of air or a string) produce a rather inharmonic series of partial tones, and bell foundries became interested in developing a shape that gave a reasonably acceptable strike tone. The blind musician and composer Jacob van Eyck (ca. 1590–1657), carillon player of the main church tower in Utrecht, discovered that the best striking clocks distinguished themselves by producing lower partials with (in modern terms) frequency ratios 5:10:12:15:20. With this "secret" he was able to instruct the bell-casting brothers François and Pieter Hemony how to correct the shape of their bells, with the result that they became the most famous bell makers in the Netherlands.[1] It is of interest to note that modern bell makers do not allow deviations greater than 1/16 semitone (0.37%), which agrees well with the 0.5% in harmonic separation, mentioned earlier, based on psychophysical testing.

TIMBRE AS THE CHARACTERISTIC QUALITY OF TONES

We have seen that although the ear analyzes sounds in terms of their sinusoidal components, the harmonics of a tone are (normally) not heard individually but fuse into a single percept, with features of pitch, loudness, and timbre. As Fig. 2.3 illustrated, the waveform of a periodic sound reflects the amplitudes of the harmonics, and perceptual tests have shown that different amplitude distributions are heard as different timbres.

However, the amplitude distribution of individual harmonics does not fully account for the waveform of a tone. According to Fourier's theorem, any waveform can be described in terms of the amplitude distribution of its harmonics, but the opposite is not the case, because very different waveforms can have the same amplitude distribution. This is a consequence of the fact that a waveform is determined not only by the amplitudes of the sinusoidal components but also by their *phases*, that is, differences in the timing of the components. Figure 2.3 represented a specific timing pattern given by the zerocrossings of the individual harmonics. Figure 2.5 illustrates that, keeping amplitude distribution constant, shifting these crossings in time (changing their phase) can result in quite different waveforms.

Thus the physical nature (waveform) of a complex tone is determined by the phases of the harmonics as well as their relative amplitudes. But does harmonic phase contribute to the perception of timbre? There is indirect evidence that this effect, if present, cannot be large. For instance, our daily experience tells us that perceived timbre is rather insensitive to our position in a room. In most cases the sound source is at such a distance that the major part of the radiated sound reaches our ears through reflections by the walls, ceiling, and so on. Their (vectorial) sum, determined by both the amplitudes and the phases of each reflected contribution, is almost unpredictable, and, depending on the position of the listener, the amplitudes of the individual harmonics can vary by more than a factor of 3, and phase relations can be completely lost. The fact that we retain a stable impression of timbre tells us not only that the effect of phase must be

---

[1]This fascinating story was studied and told by Lehr (1959).

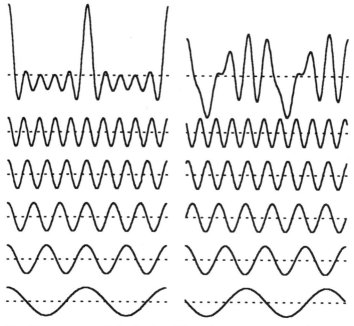

FIG. 2.5.   The upper two periodic vibrations differ exclusively in the phase relations between the five harmonics.

small or even absent, but also that the ear is rather insensitive to unrelated amplitude variations up to a factor of 3, corresponding to differences of 10 dB. Experiments have confirmed that, indeed, the effect of phase on the perception of timbre is negligible compared with the effect of amplitude (Plomp & Steeneken, 1969).

The testing of listeners' ability to differentiate timbre is more difficult than testing for pitch and loudness perception. Pitch and loudness can both be represented by one-dimensional scales, ranging from low to high and soft to loud, respectively, but differences in timbre appear to be multidimensional, depending on the amplitudes of a series of harmonics. As we have seen, the ear's frequency-analyzing power is limited to sinusoidal components differing by more than about 20%, corresponding with slightly less than $^1/_3$ octave. Only the first five harmonics of a tone are distinguishable, whereas the higher ones are not. Therefore, it seems reasonable that a spectral analysis with $^1/_3$-octave band filters is sufficient to describe the perceptually relevant differences in the tone's sound spectrum.

The significance of this reasoning is illustrated by the following example adopted from Pols, van der Kamp, and Plomp (1969). They took as stimuli single periods of 11 vowels segmented from words of the type h(vowel)t pronounced by a male speaker, equalized to have the same pitch and loudness. Two techniques were applied to obtain a multidimensional representation of the segments' spectral differences as well as of their perceptual differences.

First, the spectral differences were determined by analyzing the vowel stimuli with a series of 18 $^1/_3$-octave bandpass filters. These spectra were subjected to a principal-components analysis. The philosophy of this approach can best be illustrated geometrically by considering the 11 vowel stimuli as points in an 18-dimensional space with the sound-pressure levels of the 18 band filters as ordinates. Suppose that we have a method to find the direction in which the 11 points differ most in this multidimensional space. This is our first component, representing ("explaining") in our example 46.6% of the total variance (a measure of the spread, equal to the sum of squares of the distances of all points from their center of gravity). Similarly, a second component can be found representing the direction, perpendicular to the first one, explaining most of the remaining variance—in our case, 21.4% of the total variance. This process can be repeated to find third, fourth, and so on components accounting for less and less of the variance (third, 13.6%; fourth, 7.9%; fifth, 4.4%). Thus principal-components analysis aids in understanding the nature of the original differences. For instance, together the first two components explained 68% of the variance. This means that we can obtain a rather reliable picture of the spectral differences by considering the projection of the 11 vowels on a plane given by only the first two components. By adding additional dimensions, the accuracy can be improved.

The analysis of perceptual differences requires, of course, a quite different approach, because we can't ask listeners to map sounds into an 18-dimensional space. An attractive strategy appears to be the method of *triadic comparisons*. Listeners are presented successively with all possible triads of a stimulus set, and for each triad, they are asked to judge which pair is perceptually most different and which pair is most similar. The most different pair is assigned a score of 2 points, the most similar is assigned 0 points, and the pair remaining is given 1 point. The cumulated scores for all comparisons are then collected in a dissimilarity matrix of which the differences in cell values can be interpreted as reflecting timbre differences among the 11 stimuli. In the experiment considered here (Pols et al., 1969), such a listening test was carried out by 15 listeners. Just as a distance matrix between cities can be used to reconstruct their geographical configuration, the perceptual dissimilarity matrix can be used to find the best fitting representation of the 11 vowels. An effective method for doing this is the multidimensional scaling program developed by Kruskal (1964), which computes the best fitting configuration for the number of dimensions one wants to include.

Thus we can obtain multidimensional point configurations representing spectral differences between different sounds as well as configurations representing their perceptual dissimilarities. The final step is to compare these configurations by matching them to optimal congruence. Figure 2.6 gives the two-dimensional result for the 11 vowel stimuli considered. The correlation coefficients comparing the spectral and perceptual data are .992 for the first dimension and .971 for the second, demonstrating that there is a close relation between spectral differences for vowels measured in $^1/_3$ octaves and perceptual differences as judged by listeners. Similar results have been found for tone stimuli derived from musical instruments (Plomp, 1976).

The finding that we need only two dimensions to describe satisfactorily the differences between vowel sounds reminds us of the well-known fact that the spectra of vowels are characterized by a number of peaks or *formants*, of which the first two, usually denoted as F1 and F2, are almost sufficient to express their spectral differences (see Fig. 2.7). This being the case, it is tempting to verify whether a plane can be found in the spectral space corresponding with the F1–F2 plane. The result of this verification is shown in Fig. 2.8 (Pols, Tromp, &

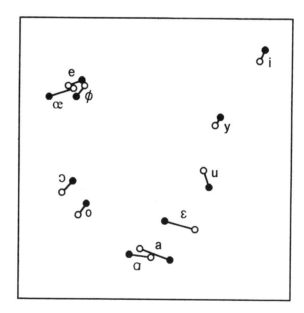

FIG. 2.6.   Result of matching in two dimensions the spectral differences (solid symbols) with the perceptual dissimilarities (open symbols) of 11 Dutch vowel sounds (Pols, van der Kamp, & Plomp, 1969).

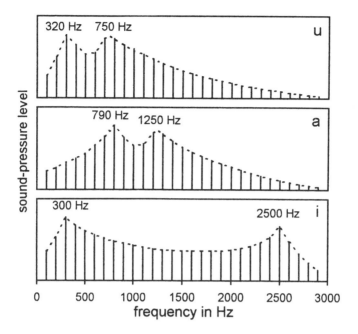

FIG. 2.7.   Spectra of the vowels /u/, /a/, and /i/, illustrating the differences in their lower two formant frequencies.

Plomp, 1973). The figure indicates that the two quite different approaches, one according to global spectral terms, the other according to specific features (the formants), are closely related. The multidimensional spectral representation covers the information given by the formant frequencies, but also contains much more information and therefore provides a more integral way to describe physically the timbre differences among vowels. In fact, as Zahorian and Jagharghi (1993) showed, the global spectral shapes are a better predictor of vowel identification than are the first three formant frequencies.

Vowels are excellent examples for demonstrating the different origins of the percepts of pitch and timbre. These two attributes of tones are essentially independent of each other. Any vowel can be spoken or sung at different pitches and yet preserves its characteristic timbre, remaining identifiable as the same vowel. In terms of speech production, this is reasonable, because the vibration frequency of the vocal chords (giving pitch) and the shape of the vocal tract (vowel spectrum) can be varied independently. However, pitch and timbre are not entirely unrelated. For the extreme case of a sinusoidal tone without harmonics, the tone's frequency as its single variable determines pitch as well as

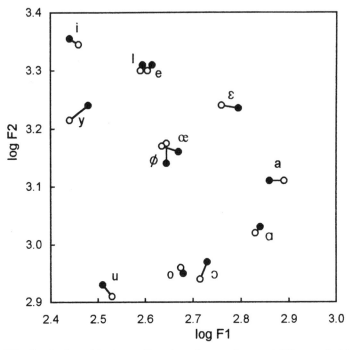

FIG. 2.8.   Result of matching in two dimensions the overall spectral differences (solid symbols) with the formant frequencies (open points) of 12 Dutch vowel sounds (Pols, Tromp, & Plomp, 1973).

timbre, with the consequence that low-pitched sinusoidal tones are described as "dull" and high-pitched tones as "sharp."

It is a general rule that the overall slope of a sound's spectrum is the main determinant of its perceived timbre, varying from dull (strong fundamental) to sharp (strong higher harmonics). This holds for vowels as well as musical tones produced by most instruments. The pipe organ represents a special case, because with this instrument it is possible to produce a large variety of different timbres by using "stops." The fundamental frequencies of these stops are multiples of the frequency of the lowest one, and thus unique tones can be created having spectra in which only certain harmonics are very salient whereas other harmonics are weak or absent. For example, the "plenum" of an organ consists of the principal stops (diapason) of the organ combined, with fundamental-frequency ratios 1:2:4:8: ... (usually expressed in the ratios of pipe lengths: 8, 4, 2, 1 feet). As the sound of diapason pipes contains mainly the first four harmonics, the combination is given by $1 : 2 : 3 : 4 : 6 : 8 : 12 : 16 : 24 : 32:....$ In contrast with a normal tone with a long series of strong harmonics, we have here a tone in which all successive harmonics differ by more than a critical bandwidth, which means that they do not interfere. This explains the uniquely sonorous "plenum" tone.

THE SEARCH FOR PITCH

The ear's frequency-analyzing process is, as explained earlier, much more complicated than one might have expected. The auditory system first resolves the sound into sinusoids but must then discover which partials were originally harmonics of the same tone. Similarly, we might suppose that determining pitch is an easy task but, again, this is not the case. Deducing the pitch of a tone is at least as complicated as deriving its timbre.

It may help to understand this difficulty by considering different solutions proposed in the past. The earliest view was that pitch is directly based on the vibration's periodicity. August Seebeck (1805–1849) may have been the first to test this general belief by means of experiments with sirens (Seebeck, 1841). He established that the repetition rate of a series of air puffs determined the pitch of the resulting sound, and he concluded that, indeed, pitch is based on periodicity. Two years later, Georg Ohm (1789–1854), well known from his famous law of electrical resistance, criticized Seebeck's conclusion (Ohm, 1843). As a strong adherent of the importance of Fourier's theorem for tone perception, Ohm held that a sinusoidal vibration with frequency f is required to hear a pitch corresponding to the frequency f. This statement became known as Ohm's definition of tone.[2]

Helmholtz agreed with Ohm and made this definition the foundation of modern hearing theory. In his informal listening experiments, Helmholtz observed that the fundamental is usually the strongest component of a tone, and he therefore concluded that pitch was derived from this partial. He believed that this is also true for tones with a weak or even missing fundamental because in those cases, he suggested, the fundamental is reintroduced as a result of the ear's nonlinearity. This view remained the prevailing theory of pitch up to the middle of the 20th century.

The first successful attack on the overriding role of the fundamental was made by Jan Schouten (1910–1980) in a series of pioneering experiments carried out in 1938–1940. Schouten generated complex tones using an optical siren, with which it was possible to cancel the fundamental completely (Schouten, 1938). The pitch of the complex tone, however, was perceived to be the same as with the

---

[2]For a more detailed review of the pitch controversy, see Plomp (1967).

fundamental present. In a subsequent paper (Schouten, 1940), he described the sensation induced by a periodic complex sound wave as follows:

> The lower harmonics can be perceived individually and have almost the same pitch as when sounded separately. The higher harmonics, however, cannot be perceived separately but are perceived collectively as one component (the residue) with a pitch determined by the periodicity of the collective wave form, which is equal to that of the fundamental tone. (p. 360)

This quotation shows that Schouten's "residue pitch" is a true "periodicity pitch" derived from the periodicity preserved in the unresolved higher harmonics. With these results, the century-old controversy regarding the basis of pitch perception came fully alive once again. In 1954 Licklider demonstrated to a meeting of the Acoustical Society of America that a melody played with complex tones does not lose its tonal character when the fundamental is completely masked by a band of noise—with this demonstration, the concept of periodicity pitch became the center of attention.

Although the argument has not been used in the past, it would be odd if the first five harmonics (usually the stronger ones) played only a minor role in pitch perception. Moreover, the fainter higher harmonics are those most susceptible to disturbing sounds. As everyday experience demonstrates, however, pitch is a very robust attribute of complex tones.

The search for the physical correlate of pitch was given further impetus by experiments reported by de Boer (1956) in which a group of neighboring harmonics was shifted in frequency. He started with a tone consisting of the harmonics,

$$800 + 1{,}000 + 1{,}200 + 1{,}400 + 1{,}600 \text{ Hz}$$

and shifted this complex over 50 Hz, resulting in

$$850 + 1{,}050 + 1{,}250 + 1{,}450 + 1{,}650 \text{ Hz}$$

For listeners, it appeared that the pitch increased from a tone with a fundamental of 200 Hz to a tone of approximately 210 Hz. Two quite different explanations of this result were proposed, depending on whether pitch is derived from the lower harmonics, which are resolved by the ear, or by the higher harmonics, which are not resolved. In the first case, the harmonics are separated by the ear and the perceived pitch can be interpreted as a *pattern-recognition* process in which a tone is "calculated" as having harmonics matching optimally the shifted series. The best choice seems to be

$$833.3 + 1{,}041.7 + 1{,}250 + 1{,}458.3 + 1{,}667.7 \text{ Hz}$$

consisting of multiples of 208.3 Hz, quite near to the observed best match. A still better agreement can be obtained by assuming that in this match lower harmonics are more important than higher ones. However, this refinement is not essential for understanding the process.[3]

The alternative explanation of the experimental finding considers the combined waveform; de Boer showed that the shift in the peaks of this waveform can explain the pitch shift reported by the listeners.

The decisive question is: Which explanation is most satisfactory? From a more practical point of view, it can be remarked that the waveform of combined harmonics is very sensitive to reflections, as discussed earlier for the effect of phase, whereas the frequencies of the harmonics are not. More basic is the question whether pitch is clearer when based on higher than on lower shifted harmonics. Extensive experimental evidence (Plomp, 1976; Ritsma, 1962) has shown that the lower harmonics, particularly the range from the third to the fifth, are most effective. Thus we may conclude that this evidence, too, argues in favor of the pattern-recognition concept.

After de Boer's experiments with five harmonics, others repeated his approach using fewer harmonics. Schouten, Ritsma, and Cardozo (1962) used stimuli consisting of three successive harmonics, and Smoorenburg (1970) and Houtsma and Goldstein (1972) employed stimuli with two harmonics. The latter investigators also included conditions in which one tone was presented to the left ear and the other to the right ear. Even in that case a pitch corresponding to the fundamental could be perceived. Finally, Houtgast (1976) tested pitch perception using only a single sinusoidal tone. By focusing a listener's attention to the frequency range around a subharmonic (e.g., around 250 Hz for a stimulus of 1,000 Hz), Houtgast found that his listeners were indeed able to hear a pitch corresponding to the subharmonic.

These additional studies are important for two reasons. In the first place, the audibility of a fundamental's pitch when the two tones are presented to different ears may be considered as strong evidence that the pitch is *not* based on the combined waveform of unresolved harmonics. This applies a fortiori for the one-tone stimuli. Thus the experimental results can be seen as additional support of the concept that the pitch of complex tones is derived from the frequencies of resolved harmonics.

---

[3]This effect was discussed in Plomp (1976).

The second reason that these studies are important concerns the sensation level at which the pitch of a series of harmonics is most easily perceived. Although most experimenters did not pay much attention to this point, they did note that low sensation levels, relative to either the hearing threshold or the masked threshold of wide-band noise, were most favorable for hearing low pitch. The most explicit statement about the effect of sensation level was given by Houtgast (1976), who compared conditions without and with added background noise:

> After the experiments the subjects commented almost unanimously that in the condition with noise all second signals [consisting of 1, 2, or 3 harmonics—RP] sounded essentially similar, with a "low pitch" (of course, different expressions were used) on which a correct response could be based; they were surprised to learn that some of these signals were in fact pure tones. However, in the series without noise, the 1-component signals were clearly identified as "just pure tones," with a complete lack of any "low-pitch" cue. (p. 407)

The observation that a low signal-to-noise ratio makes it easier to hear the pitch of a tone of which only a few successive harmonics are audible is quite interesting in light of the topics to be discussed in the next chapter. At present it may be sufficient to point out that such a sound can be interpreted as the top of a harmonically much richer tone almost completely masked by noise. Listeners appear to be able to use even such a rudiment to ascertain the pitch of the full implied tone. The higher the signal-to-noise ratio is, the more unlikely that the ear will be "misled." Other testing conditions support this view. For example, the most effective reference sounds used for perceiving the low pitch of a group of harmonics are tones with comparable timbre, and listeners are also aided if their expectations are guided. As is shown in the next chapter, the auditory system seems to be very powerful in "reconstructing" mutilated signals.

On the basis of the experimental evidence presented here as well as other findings, the pitch problem can be considered as settled. That is, the pitch of tones occurring in music and speech is primarily determined by the lower harmonics resolved by the ear. The periodicity of the unresolved higher harmonics may also contribute, but to a lesser extent (Houtsma & Smurzynski, 1990).

Traditionally, pitch perception is considered to represent the heart of hearing theory, and it is, without doubt, the topic most discussed over the years. As we saw, the mechanisms proposed vary widely. The rather recent finding that not only timbre but pitch, too, is a product of the ear's frequency-analyzing power came as a surprise. It means that in listening to two or more simultaneous complex tones—human voices at a cocktail party or the musical voices in a concert—the auditory system is continuously "testing" which sinusoidal components are harmonics of the same fundamental. The result of this sorting process "reconstructs" not only the timbres but also the pitches of the tones present. It is amazing that the process operates so quickly and reliably that we are not even aware of its existence.

THE STABILITY OF LOUDNESS

The third aspect in which tones can differ is in their loudness. Moreover, loudness is a quality in which, according to common usage, the *same* sound can vary. Timbre and pitch can be considered as inherent characteristics of a tone, whereas loudness is much less specific, strongly dependent on environmental conditions (such as distance and reflections). Loudness generally refers to auditory intensity. It seems to be the least "intelligent" attribute of sounds, and therefore our discussion of it here is short.

The loudness of a tone is primarily determined by its sound-pressure level. However, this is only a rough, first-order approximation. Two tones of the same physical intensity can still differ considerably in their perceived loudness, depending on their spectral structure. The more the intensity is spread over a wider frequency range, the louder the tone seems to be. The most extreme difference in perceived loudness is between a sinusoidal tone without harmonics and a tone consisting of a large range of strong harmonics—the sound level of the sinusoidal tone may need to be as much as 12 dB higher in order to be heard as equally loud as the complex tone.

A characteristic property of loudness is its rapid increase beyond the hearing threshold. This has been investigated by asking listeners to express the loudness of tones in numbers. Starting at a level of 10 to 20 dB above hearing threshold, an increase in level of about 9 dB is usually accepted as representing a factor two in loudness.

The most remarkable aspect of loudness manifests itself when two or more sound streams, such as two voices, are present simultaneously. We may expect that the varying extent to which they mask each other will be reflected in continuous loudness variations of the individual sounds. However, as our daily experience shows, this is not the case. We have the impression that there is no interaction between simultaneous sounds with respect to their individual loudness.

This stability can be explained partly by the fact that, as a result of the ear's frequency-resolving power, tones interact only when they are near in frequency. Figure 2.9, based on data published by Scharf (1964), illustrates how the loudness of a sinusoidal tone of variable frequency is influenced by an equally intense 160-Hz band of noise centered at 1,000 Hz. We see that this influence is

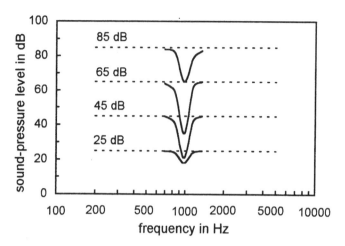

FIG. 2.9.   Sound-pressure level of a sinusoidal tone without noise, plotted as a function of frequency, sounding equally loud as tone of the same frequency presented together with a narrow band of noise centered at 1000 Hz. The loudness matching was carried out at four (equal) levels of the latter tone and the noise band (based on data from Scharf, 1964).

limited to frequencies within a quite narrow frequency range. Nevertheless, as the loudness of a tone is determined by all its harmonics together, we would expect that it is strongly affected by, for example, noise bursts masking a substantial part of its spectrum. However, that is not the case. Apparently, the hearing process, in its attempt to reconstruct the original sounds, ignores these differences in loudness. More is said about this in the next chapter.

DISCUSSION

This chapter was devoted to the three basic perceptual qualities of tones: timbre, pitch, and loudness. We found that timbre is the perceptual correlate of the waveform (representing the spectrum), pitch the correlate (but not a derivative) of the period, and loudness the correlate of the amplitude of the sound. These correspondences illustrate how closely our perception is tuned to the outer world. To a large extent the three physical parameters are independent of each other. Movements of the vocal folds determine the frequency of voiced speech sounds, whereas vocal-tract shapes create spectral distinctions between speech sounds. The same is true for musical instruments—each instrument can be used to create differences in pitch, whereas the shapes and materials used in different types of instruments give them their characteristic timbres. In all cases, the level of a sound can be varied without affecting its spectrum or periodicity.

It should be mentioned that this is a somewhat simplified picture of the psychoacoustical reality. Particularly for sinusoidal sounds, it is known that there is some pitch dependence on sound level. Also, because hearing threshold is not the same over the entire frequency range, there is a minor interdependence of timbre and loudness. However, these are second-order effects practically imperceptible in everyday situations.

Our discussion of timbre has especially been oversimplified. It cannot be assumed that the neat steady-state tone pulses of the laboratory are representative of the sounds we hear every day. Musical tones and spoken vowels are dynamic sounds that can vary substantially in time. This means that differences in timbre are not fully accounted for by spectral differences. The significance of additional parameters has been demonstrated convincingly for musical tones. For example, Iverson and Krumhansl (1993) compared the timbre contribution of the onsets of orchestral instrument tones with the contribution of the remainder of the tones. Their finding that both contributions are roughly comparable demonstrates the substantial role of dynamic factors, most manifest in onset differences between the string and wind instruments. Sustained notes from a violin and a trumpet are spectrally quite similar, but we hear them as very different sounds due primarily to the dynamic properties of their onsets.

Another question not addressed in this chapter is the role of nonlinear distortion in hearing, the phenomenon where the output amplitude of a signal is not exactly proportional to the input amplitude. Since Helmholtz's extensive discussion of the nonlinearity of the ear's mechanical sound transmission (von Helmholtz, 1863/1954), the topic has received substantial attention. Such a nonlinearity manifests itself in the creation of new tones not present in the input signal. For example, a sinusoidal tone with frequency f produces tones with frequencies nf, and two tones with frequencies f_1 and f_2 $(f_2 > f_1)$ interact resulting in new tones with frequencies $mf_1 - nf_2$ (where m, n are integers). Particularly in the 1960s these combination tones were studied intensively, with interest also stimulated by their supposed role in the audibility of beats for slightly mistuned pairs of tones.[4] It appeared that $2f_1 - f_2$ can be rather strong for small values of $f_2 - f_1$. This would indicate that simultaneous tones, as in music, strongly interact. However, although our ears are very sensitive to nonlinear distortion in the form of intermodulation in sound-transmission systems, resulting in a reduced "transparency" of the music, this has not been shown to be the case for distortions introduced by the ear itself. This remarkable discrepancy in the perception of externally versus internally originating distortion has still not been explored properly.

---

[4]The occurrence of combination tones and beats was discussed extensively in Plomp (1976).

In addition, detection thresholds, another favorite topic of a few decades ago, did not receive much attention here. Detection thresholds, whether or not expressed in the d' of signal-detection theory, are useful for describing the limits of the auditory system's capacity, but they do not represent the *essence* of the perception process. Just-noticeable differences in frequency, amplitude, and so on can inform us about *whether* differences between sounds are perceived, but they do not inform us about the attributes of *what* is perceived, without doubt the much more important question.

As we have seen, the process of analyzing sounds into their spectral components is an essential stage in auditory perception, but it is only the first stage. An artificial system could be designed to do exactly the same. But this apparatus would be unable to reconstruct the original sounds from the sinusoidal components and to characterize them according to their timbre and pitch. Both analysis and synthesis are required to perform this task. Hence, we may say that the auditory system is a quite unique sound analyzer.

Of all the phenomena discussed in this and the following chapters, the ones described in the present chapter have been most studied physiologically. However, even here, our knowledge is almost exclusively limited to the ear's frequency-resolving power. More than a century ago, Helmholtz (von Helmholtz, 1863/1954) exerted much effort to convince his readers that the cochlea is a frequency analyzer. In his view, the basilar membrane within the cochlea, extending over (almost) its entire length, should be seen as a series of strings tuned from low to high frequency much like the strings of a piano. Modern research, initiated by Georg von Békésy's (1899–1972) first successful attempts to observe the membrane's movements, has abandoned the idea of vibrating strings in favor of the concept of traveling waves with a frequency-dependent peak along the basilar membrane (von Békésy, 1960). This means that Helmholtz's view locating frequency analysis in the peripheral ear was essentially correct. Animal studies have abundantly demonstrated that the individual nerve fibers associated with the hair cells along the basilar membrane transfer faithfully the results of the peripheral frequency analysis to higher centers in the auditory pathway.

Our physiological knowledge of how sounds are processed does not extend significantly beyond this first stage of frequency analysis. Subsequent processes are clearly required to group components originally belonging to the same sound, to characterize the sound's timbre, to "compute" pitch, and to mark loudness. It is obvious that these all are neural processes depending on the electrical inputs of large numbers of neurons. Up to now, no physiologically based description of these processes has been made. Such a description would be particularly intriguing for the pitch processor, which is surely a rather sophisticated mechanism. Only speculations based on algorithms are available.

The fact that in listening to a mixture of sounds both the pitch and timbre of each individual sound are so readily perceived demonstrates that our hearing is, even in its most elementary processes, aimed at undoing the unavoidable consequences of the fact that all incoming sounds are superimposed in the air. We hear these individual sounds as if they had never been mixed. Hearing, even at its most elementary level, is clearly the result of highly "intelligent" processes operating so well that extensive hearing research was required to discover their existence. This is all the more true for the perceptual separation of series of successive sounds, considered in the next chapter.

CONCLUSIONS

We have seen in this chapter that the ear and auditory system represent a rather unique frequency-analyzing system. This system manages to separate sounds entering the ear canal so perfectly by source, it is as if the sounds had reached the ear through different channels rather than as a superimposed air vibration. This means that the peripheral ear, working as a straightforward frequency analyzer, is followed by a second, neural, stage in which the spectral components originally belonging to the same sound are reunited in a single percept. Specific processes must be employed resulting in the perception of timbre as the counterpart of the sound's spectrum, pitch as the counterpart of its periodicity, and loudness as the counterpart of its sound level.

3
The Perception of Multiple Sounds

The previous chapter presented a brief exposition of how timbre, pitch, and loudness as the main perceptual attributes of single sounds are derived from periodic vibrations. It may seem that with these attributes we have obtained a reasonably complete picture of how tones are perceived. However, this conclusion would be rather premature. This chapter shows that there are unique auditory processes that are crucially important for dealing with the simultaneous sounds from many sources in our everyday environment. Such sounds may be from competing speakers, musical instruments of an orchestra, cars in the street, and so on. Their vibrations are superimposed in the air and, in order to obtain a reliable impression of what is going on around us, we must be able to distinguish the individual sounds as well as possible. Without appropriate perceptual processing, listeners would find that a speaker became immediately unintelligible as soon as a second speaker joined the conversation, and polyphonic music would be impossible. We might compare this with the difficulty of reading a text from a sheet of paper on which a second text had been written.

Fortunately, our ingenious auditory system is not only able to sort out which fragments of sounds originate from which source, but also to *reconstruct* the individual sounds as if they were never superimposed. The fragments of each sound, be it a voice, the tone of a violin, or the noise of a train, are heard as a continuous, distinct sound stream as if never mixed with the other simultaneous sounds. Just as with many other perceptual processes, such as constancy of size, shape, and color in vision, the auditory reconstruction process is so perfect that we are normally not aware of its existence. It had to be "discovered" in the laboratory in order to get attention. Even so, it took some time before the fundamental role of this process in hearing was generally recognized and for the conditions under which it is evoked to become a topic for systematic studies.

In this chapter some principal results are reviewed demonstrating the sophisticated strategies our auditory system employs for handling multiple simultaneous sounds. For reasons of clarity, this discussion is almost exclusively based on experiments with nonsimultaneous sounds consisting of successive segments, which listeners perceive as either a single stream or two (or more) independent streams, depending on their properties.

THE CONTINUITY EFFECT

In 1950, Miller and Licklider published an article on the intelligibility of interrupted speech, in which they referred to a phenomenon which had not been described before. They noted that if a tone is interrupted 10 to 15 times per second, the "interrupted tone will sound quite pure and continuous if the intervals between the bursts of tone are filled with a sufficiently intense white noise" (p. 173). Some years later, Thurlow (1957), apparently independently, reported a variant of this observation:

> In exploring the effects obtained with two alternately sounding tones we found an auditory effect which may be regarded as a figure-ground phenomenon. Under certain conditions, the more intense of the two tones is heard as clearly intermittent (somewhat as "figure"), and the less intense appears to sound continuously (somewhat as "ground"). In a sense this is analogous to the situation in vision, where the ground is perceived as extending continuously behind the figure. (p. 653)

In this study Thurlow was using tone pulses of 4,000 Hz, duration 60 msec, sensation level 60 dB, alternating with tone pulses of 3,000 Hz, duration 40 msec, sensation level 45 dB. This *continuity effect* was further explored in subsequent papers (e.g., Elfner & Homick, 1967; Thurlow & Elfner, 1959), revealing that the effect is limited to conditions where the weaker tones are similar in frequency to the louder tones. The discovery of the continuity effect did not arouse any immediate interest outside the circle of its initiators.

It was not until 20 years later that the continuity effect began to attract more attention. In the 1970s, Warren rediscovered the effect and gave it a new name: *auditory induction* (Warren, Obusek, & Ackroff, 1972). This paper ended with the conclusion:

> Auditory induction appears to be a quite useful perceptual phenomenon permitting a highly selective reinstatement of sounds which would otherwise be lost through masking. The listener can thus establish a simpler and more stable interpretation of his auditory environment than the intermittent extraneous sounds present in our noisy world would otherwise permit. (p. 1151)

This is a very modest formulation of what is actually one of the most fundamental properties of the auditory system. Thanks to it, we are able to hear a voice or a musical melody, even when it is competing with another simultaneous sound, as a continuous stream rather than as a series of intermittent segments.

Beginning with Warren, then, interest in the continuity effect increased considerably. Houtgast (1973) studied it within the framework of the phenomenon of lateral suppression of one tone by another. He alternated a louder tone with a weaker tone, both having a duration of 125 msec, and, by varying the frequency of the weaker tone, he was able to determine the threshold value at which the weaker tone was heard as continuous rather than pulsating. In Fig. 3.1 this *pulsation threshold* is plotted for fixed louder tones of 300, 1,000, and 3,000 Hz.

Note that these peaked curves, bordering the area within which the weaker tone pulses sound as a continuous tone, resemble the selectivity curves of Fig. 2.1. Those curves represented the maximal sound-pressure level of a simultaneously presented probe tone that resulted in a just-perceptible increase of neural activity. Similarly, we may assume that the nonsimultaneously presented weaker tone pulses will be heard as a continuous tone if the neural activity they evoke does not exceed the activity created by the louder tone pulses. Apparently, under these conditions, the auditory system cannot determine whether the weaker tone was continuously present or not. As a result, it opts for the former alternative as the more likely solution, resulting in a kind of gestalt continu-

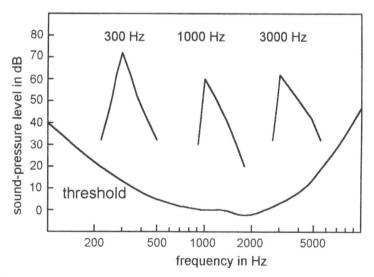

FIG. 3.1. Pulsation threshold of tones of 300 Hz, 1000 Hz, and 3000 Hz. The lower curve represents the absolute hearing threshold (based on data from Houtgast, 1973).

ation judgement. In this respect this perceptual effect might be compared to the sensation aroused by sitting in a standing train and seeing another train starting to move. Invariably the impression is that our train rather than the other train is moving. Again, the system opts for the more likely condition, in this visual case a stationary world in which the observer is assumed to be moving.

The continuity effect is, as said, a major feature of auditory perception, and we must realize that it represents a much more radical phenomenon than the visual illusion just mentioned. Given what we know about the synchronization of nerve impulses to the period of the sound vibration, it is certain that nerve fibers in the cochlea undergo very different stimulation for each of the two tones. Nevertheless, we seem to hear the weaker tone continuing during the periods when actually only the louder tone is present. Thus a single sequence of sounds is perceived as two independent sound streams. The auditory system judges the weaker tone pulses to be parts of a continuous tone, and perceptually restores the parts "covered up" by the louder tone bursts—in other words, there is a perceptual *(re-)creation* of sounds on the basis of probability. We may conclude that this restoration is the result of an active "intelligent" process, especially aimed at reconstructing and preserving the original properties of a sound radiated from a source that is assumed to be continuous, irrespective of interfering sounds.

The continuity effect has been demonstrated for a wide range of interruption rates between 75 and 200 msec (Verschuure, Rodenburg, & Maas, 1976). As the following chapters show, this range covers the duration of individual vowels and consonants as well as most syllables. The significance of the effect for speech perception is discussed in the third section of this chapter, but first we consider some further findings using tonal stimuli.

Up to now, we have only considered the case of tones with fixed frequency. Some scientists have tried to explain the continuity effect as an aftereffect comparable with afterimages in vision. If this explanation were correct, continuity should be lost for tones that vary in frequency. Take, for example, the case where a gliding tone, increasing from 500 to 2,000 Hz, is periodically interrupted and the gaps are filled with louder noise covering the frequency band of 900 to 1,100 Hz. Figure 3.2 illustrates this condition. A listener will hear separate tone pulses as long as the tone frequency is below 900 Hz or above 1,100 Hz, but as the tone passes through the frequency range covered by the noise band, the tone appears to continue, with a continuously rising pitch. This demonstrates that the perception of continuity is not based on an auditory afterimage but must be considered as an active restoration of a predicted, most probable course of the tone during the noise bursts.

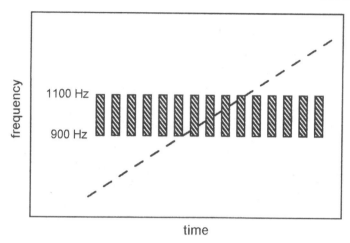

FIG. 3.2.   A tone varying from 500 Hz to 2000 Hz, alternated four times per sec with a noise band between 900 Hz and 1100 Hz, is heard over this frequency range continuously as a gliding tone.

Bregman and coworkers at McGill University in Montreal have been responsible for much of the research on the continuity effect. The effect forms the nucleus of Bregman's monograph entitled *Auditory Scene Analysis*, published in 1990. Building on earlier work by Dannenbring (1976), Ciocca and Bregman (1987) studied the perceived continuity of gliding and steady-state tones differing in frequency and/or rate of frequency shift, presented before and after a louder 150-msec noise burst. The heavy lines in Fig. 3.3 represent results for each of the three cases (A, B, and C): The three gliding tones after the noise burst are heard as most continuous—persisting straight through the noise—with the tones prior to the noise burst. The auditory system "expects" that a descending pitch either will continue to descend, or will be followed by an ascending pitch, or vice versa, whereas a constant pitch is expected to remain constant.

Similarly, the continuity effect holds for complex tones consisting of a series of harmonics of which a number are alternated with louder noise. Figure 3.4A illustrates the case where the higher harmonics of a complex tone are periodically interrupted and replaced by noise. Figure 3.4B represents a much more radical form of interruption in which the lower and higher harmonics are alternately replaced by noise in such a way that the two subsets are never present simultaneously. Irrespective of whether or not listeners know the composition of the stimuli, they are convinced that they hear in both cases a *continuous* complex tone plus a separate stream of noise bursts. This demonstrates clearly that

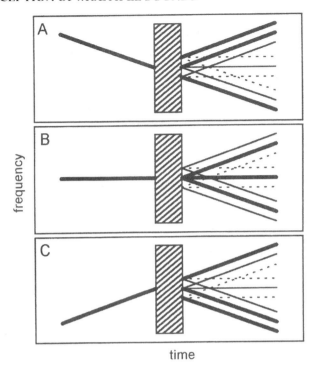

FIG. 3.3. The lines represent the frequencies of tones presented before and after a noise burst of 150 millisec. The heavy lines after the burst are the tones heard as most continuous, the dashed lines as the tones least continuous with the tones prior to the burst (based on data from Ciocca & Bregman, 1987).

all three principal tone attributes of timbre, pitch, and loudness are involved in the restoration process.

Another interesting issue is what we hear when a melodic sequence of tones rather than a gliding tone is periodically interrupted by noise bursts overlapping the transitions between successive tones, destroying the rhythm of the pulses. Figure 3.5 represents such a case in which tone pulses of 250 msec are interrupted by 150-msec noise bursts, such that all except the first two noise bursts cover a tonal transition. Yet the melody is heard as if it had not been disturbed. However, in this case, expectations can change the perception. For example, by first listening repeatedly to the tone pulses with the noise bursts replaced by silent intervals (Fig. 3.5B), listeners can be trained to expect a much more complex rhythm, with the result that the practiced rhythm is heard even when the noise bursts are reintroduced (Fig. 3.5A). This is a nice illustration of *hearing what we expect to hear.*

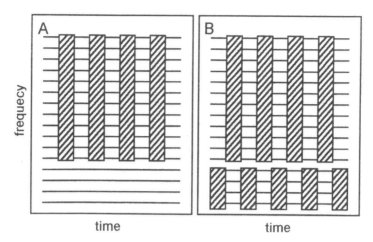

FIG. 3.4.   The lines represent the harmonics of a tone partly alternated with noise bursts. In panel A, the lower harmonics are presented continuously, in panel B, the lower and higher harmonics are presented alternately.

In all these examples, periodic interruptions were used, but this is not essential for perceptual continuity. The effect is just as strong for irregular interruptions, as long as they occur within the range of 75 to 200 msec already mentioned.

SEGREGATION OF A SEQUENCE OF SOUNDS INTO TWO SOUND STREAMS

The loudness difference between the two sets of alternating sounds in the previous section was essential for listeners to hear the weaker tone as continuing straight through the louder tones or noise bursts. But what occurs when two tones differing in frequency but approximately equal in loudness are alternated? Miller and Heise (1950) were the first to report that if the frequency difference is small, the tone pulses are heard as a coherent sequence of tones with the pitch going up and down periodically, but as the frequency difference is made larger, the coherence disappears and the series of tones splits up into two streams, one consisting of the lower frequency tones, the other of the higher frequency tones (see Fig. 3.6).

In a subsequent study (Heise & Miller, 1951), this phenomenon was tested for sequences of eleven 125-msec repeatedly presented tone pulses, with all frequencies fixed except the sixth pulse. The listeners were asked to adjust the frequency of the sixth pulse to such a value that it just separated perceptibly (i.e., appeared in a different stream) from the other ones. The solid points in Fig. 3.7

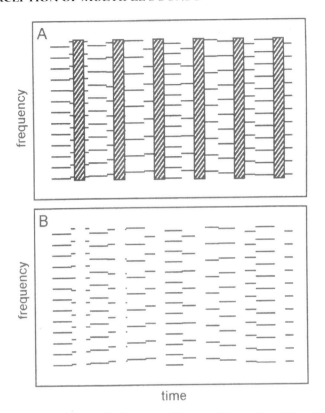

FIG. 3.5.   The lines represent the harmonics of a series of tone pulses with varying pitch. Panel A shows the tones interrupted by noise bands of which the latter four cover transitions from one tone to the next. Despite this temporal uncertainty, the tones are heard as a melody of equally lasting tones. By listening first repeatedly to the tone pulses *without* noise (panel B) the rhythm heard *with* noise adapts to this condition.

give three examples of these fixed-pulse sequences, with the separation thresh-old of the variable sixth pulse represented by the open points. These diagrams il-lustrate that hearing all tones as a single stream depends on the frequency pattern of the entire series of tones.

It is evident that perceptual streaming plays an important role in music. Composers long ago discovered the phenomenon and have often exploited it in compositions. For example, Johann Sebastian Bach depended on listeners' streaming ability to suggest two melody lines in his Partita Nr. 3 for solo violin in E major.

The phenomenon was also studied extensively by van Noorden (1975) in his doctoral thesis, from which most data discussed next are taken. Figure 3.8

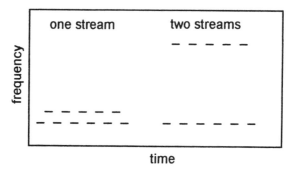

FIG. 3.6.   Successive tone pulses with a small frequency difference are heard as a single sound stream, while pulses with a large frequency difference are heard as two independent streams.

shows that there is a wide range of frequency differences within which a single coherent sound stream as well as two separated streams may be heard. As the author wrote:

> It would seem as if the percepts are mutually exclusive in the perception. When one listens without special attention, one hears first the one percept and then the other. The change-over is then spontaneous, and appears to occur at random moments. (p. 9)

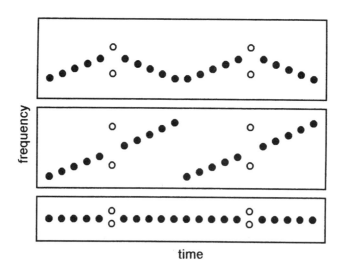

FIG. 3.7.   The panels illustrate that hearing a tone pulse (open symbol) as not belonging to a series of successive tone pulses (solid symbols) depends on the frequency pattern (based on data from Heise & Miller, 1951).

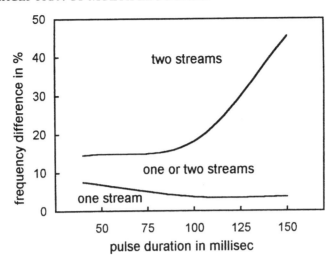

FIG. 3.8.   Frequency difference for which pulses of a higher tone, alternated with pulses of 1000 Hz, are heard as one stream or as two streams (based on data from van Noorden, 1975).

Thus this instance of auditory streaming bears a striking resemblance to "visual streaming" of shapes, such as the faces/vase visual illusion.

Van Noorden found that although the lower boundary of mixed range where both percepts can occur is rather independent of pulse duration, the upper boundary increases considerably for longer tone pulses. Streaming breaks down for tones longer than about 200 msec, which are perceived as independent from each other rather than as a pattern.

The boundary curves in Fig. 3.8 are for repeatedly alternating tone pulses, and represent the optimal condition for hearing two streams. Subsequent data reported by van Noorden indicate that if tone sequences are shorter, the frequency difference between tones can be larger and still permit streaming. In the extreme case of only two tone pulses per sequence, a very much larger frequency difference can be tolerated than in the case of multiple pulses. This can be verified easily with 100-msec pulses having a frequency ratio of 2:3; the two tone pulses of a single pair sound as though they belong to each other as a melodic interval, but this quality quickly disappears if the pair is repeated over and over without pauses.

This dependence of the stream-segregation boundary on the length of the sequence can be interpreted as indicating that previous tones play a role in the grouping process by biasing expectations. Beauvois and Meddis (1997) studied this bias effect by presenting listeners with an initial 10 sec of repeated 1,000-Hz tone pulses. Subsequently, after a variable silent period, a sequence of eight tone pulses, alternating between 1,000 Hz and 1,420 Hz, was presented. The results indicated that the alternating pulses were much more frequently heard as segregating when presented after a short silent period than when presented after a long period. Apparently, the system's "conclusion" that the four deviating pulses of 1,420 Hz could not belong to the sequence faded gradually as a function of time.

An unexpected streaming pattern occurs when a sequence of tone pulses with increasing frequency is alternated with a sequence of tones with decreasing frequency (see Fig. 3.9). One might expect that the two sequences would seem to "pass" each other in a similar way as visual patterns do, represented in the left panel by different line thickness. However, van Noorden observed that this is not the case: The melodies do not "cross" but instead segregate into a higher and a lower melody (visualized in the right panel).

In the experiments described so far, sinusoidal tones were used. However, the coherence of tone sequences depends on timbre as well as pitch. A striking demonstration can be given by replacing one of the two crossing sequences of pulses with complex tones. Even a single harmonic is sufficient to hear the two sequences as actually crossing (indicated by the lines in the left panel of Fig. 3.9).

Another example of the role of timbre is illustrated in Fig. 3.10. The three panels represent three different conditions investigated by van Noorden. In the case on the left, a sinusoidal tone is alternated with a complex tone comprised of the third to the 10th harmonics of the tone. Both tones have, as we saw in chapter 2, the same pitch but they differ considerably in timbre. As a consequence of this difference, these tone pulses are not heard as a coherent stream. The middle panel of Fig. 3.10 illustrates the case where alternating tone pulses represent three harmonics of the same fundamental frequency. Again, the repeated tone pulses are heard as two streams. For the case shown in the right panel, the three pulses differ slightly in fundamental frequency, and consequently in harmonics,

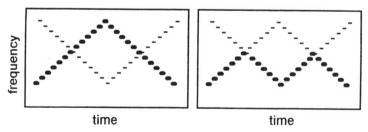

FIG. 3.9.   Two sequences of alternating tone pulses crossing each other in frequency are only heard as crossing (panel A) if they differ in timbre; if not, they segregate in a lower and a higher melody (panel B).

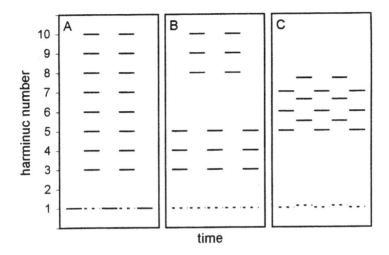

FIG. 3.10. Panel A represents a sinusoidal tone alternating with a complex tone of the same pitch but different timbre (harmonics 3–10 only); Panel B, two alternating complex tones of the same pitch but different timbre (harmonics 3–5 vs. 8–10 only); Panel C, two alternating complex tones differing slightly in pitch and timbre (both harmonics 5–7 only). Conditions A and B are heard as two streams; condition C heard as one. The dashes represent the (absent) fundamental.

but such that the differences in pitch as well as in timbre are small. In this third case the tone pulses fuse into a single stream.

These observations demonstrate clearly that there are rather strict conditions under which successive sounds of short durations are perceived as a coherent sound stream. The pitch, timbre, and loudness of segments are very important to the effect—none should differ much from segment to segment. This certainly suggests that the auditory system is deciding whether or not the successive sounds had their origins in the same source or different sources. Small variations over time may be possible for a single source, but large changes may signal the presence of two (or more) sources.

This highly sophisticated way of processing illustrates again that the auditory system is fully equipped to separate superimposed sounds. It does not accept "naively" the incoming sounds as a sequence of independent events, as a mechanical analyzer would do. The goal of perception is clearly aimed at finding structure in the sounds, and grouping them according to criteria that match the nature of sound sources in the real world. Thus we see that sound perception is governed primarily by holistic rather than elementalistic principles.

RESTORATION OF SPEECH SEGMENTS
REPLACED BY NOISE

As we saw in the first section of this chapter, the continuity effect for tones was first reported by Miller and Licklider (1950) in a paper on the intelligibility of interrupted speech, addressing the question of economizing speech transmission. It is well known that the redundancy of the speech signal allows a substantial reduction in signal bandwidth with no loss of intelligibility. But how acceptable would it be to introduce temporal rather than spectral reduction in speech? An obvious manipulation would be to interrupt the speech signal periodically. Miller and Licklider found that for lists of words, there was a broad maximum in the intelligibility score around 10 to 20 interruptions per second, and this was almost irrespective of the on–off ratio. They also examined the effect of introducing noise in the silent intervals for an on–off ratio of 1 (speech present 50% of the time). Figure 3.11 gives the results as a function of the speech-to-noise ratio. The effect of the noise is most severe for high interruption rates. This can be explained by the occurrence of aftermasking, that is, masking that persists every time that the noise is stopped. As a consequence, the noise shifts the intelligibility peak to lower rates, but keeps it still very pronounced. From this figure we may conclude that, even when relatively strong noise bursts are used, sentences alternating with noise 10 times per second are still quite intelligible.

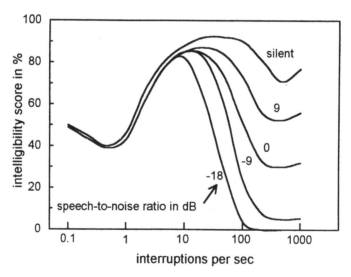

FIG. 3.11.   Word identification score as a function of alternation rate between speech and noise, with speech-to-noise ratio as the parameter (redrawn from Miller & Licklider, 1950).

Within the framework of this chapter, Miller and Licklider's comments in the last paragraph of their paper are most important:

> An interesting effect is observed if noise is introduced into the gaps between bursts of speech when the speech is interrupted about 10 to 15 times per second. Without the noise the talker's voice sounds hoarse and raucous. The speech is intelligible, but the interruptions are quite evident. When noise is introduced between the bursts of speech, the on and off transients are assimilated into the noise and, when the noise is somewhat more intense than the speech, the speech begins to sound continuous and uninterrupted. It is much like seeing a landscape through a picket fence—the pickets interrupt the view at regular intervals, but the landscape is perceived as continuing behind the pickets. (p. 173)

We have seen previously that interruptions of tones can be perceptually restored by the introduction of noise in the silent gaps, and this observation indicates that the same is also true for interrupted speech. A demonstration of this by Warren (1970) has received much attention in the literature. In the sentence "The state governors met with their respective legislatures convening in the capitol city," he replaced the first "s" in "legislatures" with a 120-msec louder cough and asked listeners to mark the position of the cough on a typed version of the sentence. Nineteen out of 20 subjects reported that all phonemes were present and none of them could correctly identify the identity or location of the missing phoneme. (This issue of temporal uncertainty is considered again in the next section.) Warren suggested the term *phonemic restoration* for this phenomenon. Just as with tones, the restoration phenomenon in speech requires that the level of the replacement noise exceeds the level of the speech over the entire frequency range (Bashford & Warren, 1987).

At the end of the paragraph partially quoted, Miller and Licklider made the intriguing remark that their listeners reported that noise in the silent interval not only made the speech sound more natural but also "probably more intelligible," although this impression is not supported by the curves in Fig. 3.11. Powers and Wilcox (1977) tested this and found in fact that the intelligibility score for sentences that were interrupted 1.5 times per second with an on–off ratio of 1, increased significantly when noise was introduced in the gaps, reaching a maximum around a speech-to-noise ratio of –20 dB. The fact that this rather large level difference can be tolerated is explained by the caveat that the loudness of the noise has to exceed the loudness of the interrupted sound *over the entire frequency range* if listeners are to perceive continuity. The discrepancy between the two studies with respect to the effect of introducing noise in the silent gaps can be explained by the differences in speech materials used: Miller and Licklider presented words, whereas Powers and Wilcox used meaningful sentences that are, owing to their redundancy, much more resistant to interference (Bashford, Riener, & Warren, 1992; Verschuure & Brocaar, 1983).

Figure 3.11 presented the range of interruption rates over which the introduction of noise is most effective in terms of intelligibility score, but does not indicate how long the gaps can be and the missing speech still be restored. Bashford and Warren (1987) concluded that maximal interruption-gap length depends on the nature of the speech material, ranging from about 150 msec for monosyllables to approximately the length of a word (250–300 msec) for meaningful sentences.

Phonemic restoration is not restricted to the condition where speech is periodically alternated with louder bursts of noise. Cherry and Wiley (1967) reported an experiment in which weaker portions of a speech passage were edited out. Adding white noise into these gaps had a striking effect on the mutilated speech, restoring an impression of naturalness. Hollaway (1970) measured intelligibility under the same conditions and found that the added noise increased intelligibility scores.

A second variant of this manipulation, but involving spectral rather than temporal gaps, was studied more recently by Warren et al. (1997). Sentences were processed through two extremely narrow band filters (1/20 octave = 3.5%; slopes of 115 dB/octave) centered at 370 and 6,000 Hz, and the spectral gap in between was filled with a matching noise band. Again, the noise replacing the absent speech band improved the intelligibility score, and there was a distinctly optimal noise level.

These experiments provide further evidence that hearing is not a passive but a very active process. Tones, speech, or other sounds may seem to be disturbed by interfering sounds but the system appears to have effective ways of reconstructing the original sound. Even for short speech segments, this process is so effective that we are not aware of its existence.

PERCEIVING TEMPORAL ORDER

When a listener's percept changes from hearing alternating tone pulses as a single stream for small frequency differences, to two streams for large frequency differences, this is accompanied by a second perceptual effect. Subjects tested by van Noorden (1975) reported that when a tone sequence loses its coherence in this way, it becomes impossible to perceive the order or precise relative temporal relation of the two segregated series of tone pulses.

This phenomenon was studied quantitatively by van Noorden for two alternating sequences of 50-msec tone pulses as a function of the repetition time of the successive pulses as well as their frequency difference. The curves in Fig. 3.12 represent the just-noticeable temporal shift of the two pulse series expressed as percentage of repetition time; the parameter of the curves is the frequency ratio of the tones. We see that for repetition times up to about 120 msec, corresponding with the range of strong segregation (see Fig. 3.8), the sensitivity to temporal differences is indeed much smaller than for large repetition times, where the coherence depends much less upon frequency ratio.

In a subsequent experiment, van Noorden compared this condition of continuously repeated tone pulses with the condition where a single pair of 50-msec tone pulses differing in frequency was followed 500 msec later by a second pair, used as a reference. Figure 3.13 shows that, for equal repetition times of 100 msec, the single pair is much more sensitive to a temporal shift than the continuously repeated pulses. This may seem a curious result, but it agrees perfectly with the earlier mentioned observation that a single pair of tones can sound much more coherent than repeated pulses.

More complex sounds have also been studied in this way. Warren and Warren (1970) created sequences consisting of 200-msec pulses of a high-pitched tone, a square wave, a low-pitched tone, and a band of noise. When these sounds were continuously repeated in a loop, listeners were unable to identify the order of the sounds. Sound segments had to be lengthened to 300–700 msec before order could be determined. On the other hand, the order of four

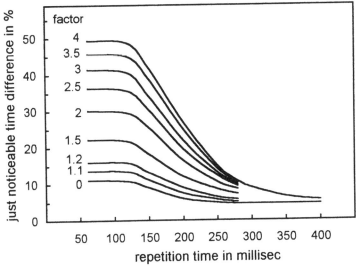

FIG. 3.12. Just-noticeable time difference between two series of alternating tone pulses (lower tone 1000 Hz) as a function of repetition time, with frequency ratio as the parameter (redrawn from van Noorden, 1975).

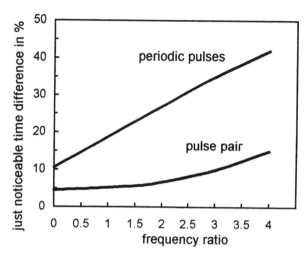

FIG. 3.13. Just-noticeable time difference between two series of alternating tone pulses (lower tone 1000 Hz) compared with a single pulse pair (redrawn from van Noorden, 1975).

200-msec digit names was always correctly identified. When the experiment was repeated a third time using four 200-msec vowel segments edited from sustained real vowels, again listeners could not label the order. Replacing 50 msec of the abutting vowels by silent gaps (to make them more speechlike) increased scores from chance to about 50%. Performance approached 100% only if each sustained vowel segment was edited to have normal onsets and decays. Based on these findings, it may be very tempting to conclude (as several investigators have done) that speech and nonspeech are differently perceived. However, this question can only be answered after considering the following points:

1. *The significance of smooth transitions.* In the case of van Noorden's tonal stimuli (Fig. 3.10), it was clear that sounds fuse into a single stream only if their spectra do not differ much, so that they resemble each other in pitch as well as in timbre and loudness. In addition, the introduction of smooth transitions in the pauses between sound segments appears to promote streaming, as has been shown for tone pulses (Bregman & Dannenbring, 1973) as well as for vowel sounds (Cole & Scott, 1973; Dorman, Cutting, & Raphael, 1975).

2. *Task demands: discrimination versus identification.* A same–different discrimination between different sequences of short sounds appears to be much easier than naming their temporal order. Warren (1974) observed that when listeners were allowed to judge same–different, they could quite readily discriminate loops composed of the four nonspeech stimuli differing only in the order of the square wave and noise. Similar results were observed for sequences of four dif-

ferent tones arranged in all six possible orders (Warren & Byrnes, 1975). In this case, subjects could distinguish the repeated sequences even for pulse durations as short as 50 msec, where temporal order identification was completely impossible. Apparently, the difficulty lies not in the perception but in the naming.

3. *"Endless" repetition versus single presentation.* It is obviously artificial to present the same sequence of sounds again and again as a loop rather than as a single event. The nature of this repetition with its associated strong segregation effects makes it difficult to extract temporal order and is, of course, not representative of the speech signal with its continuously changing structure. Warren (1974) repeated his experiment using two different sequences of four unrelated stimuli (pure tone/noise/square wave/pure tone *vs.* pure tone/square wave/noise/pure tone), with only one sequence presented per trial, and obtained completely different results. Even for segment durations as short as 10 msec, more than 90% of the sequences were correctly identified. Still better scores were obtained after removing the tone pulses so that only square wave and noise pulses were left. As Warren noted, these results do not mean that the subjects had learned to perceive the temporal order of the very short stimuli. Rather, they heard the sequences as an acoustically complex pattern and had learned to label their global perceptual difference. In the same way, being able to name the order of the individual phonemes of a word may be understood as the result of a second-stage analysis based on recognition of the word as a whole. A good illustration is given by the performance of listeners tested by Dorman, Cutting, and Raphael (1975), who "recognized," for example, the vowel sequence /i, æ, u, æ/ as /yæwæ/, an indirect way to identify temporal order without having it actually observed. This conclusion drawn from experimental results is entirely in agreement with views about how we perceive syllables and words in general, discussed in the following chapters.

These three points combined provide ample evidence that basic perceptual rules can account for the fact that we perceive fluent speech as a single stream of sound without having to identify explicitly the order of phonemes.

THE SEEMINGLY ODD PHENOMENON OF COMODULATION MASKING RELEASE

Figure 3.13 showed that the perception of a single pulse pair is much more sensitive to a shift in timing than for repeated pulses. I called this a seemingly curious phenomenon because it clashes with the (preferred) elementalistic way of thinking. Another, even more striking, example of counterintuitive perceptual behavior is comodulation masking release, described for the first time by Hall,

Haggard, and Fernandes (1984). Here I explain this phenomenon as exemplified in a later experiment.

Grose and Hall (1989) studied the effect of amplitude modulation of a continuous complex tone on the detectability of a tone pulse. The complex tone consisted of the harmonics of 300, 400, 500, … , 1,100 Hz of an (absent) 100-Hz fundamental frequency. The amplitude of this signal was sinusoidally modulated at 10 Hz. The modulation depth was varied in steps between 0% and 100%, and for each step the detection threshold of a 250-msec tone pulse of 700 Hz was measured. The stimulus configuration is illustrated in Fig. 3.14. Figure 3.15 gives the average detection threshold for six test subjects as a function of modulation depth. For 100% modulation, the threshold is 14 dB lower than for 0% modulation.

At first glance this result should not surprise us. Varying the amplitude of all harmonics, including the one at 700 Hz, increases the chance that the target tone pulses of that frequency will become audible during the modulation val-

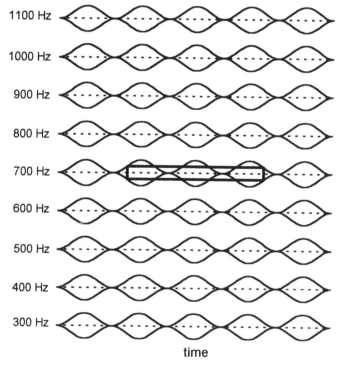

FIG. 3.14.   Stimulus configuration for 100% modulation in the experiment by Grose and Hall (1989). The rectangle at 700 Hz represents the target stimulus.

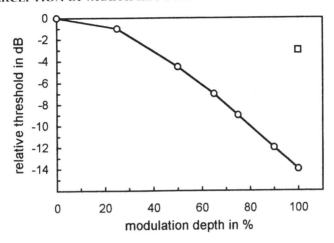

FIG. 3.15.   Detection threshold of a 700-Hz tone pulse as a function of the modulation depth of the nine harmonics of the masking sound. The square symbol represents the threshold when only the 100% modulated component of 700 Hz is present (redrawn from Grose & Hall, 1989).

leys. If this explanation is correct, we should expect the same 14-dB gain if only the harmonic of 700 Hz is presented. However, the square symbol in Fig. 3.15 shows that this is not the case. With only the 700-Hz harmonic present, threshold at 100% modulation was only about 3 dB lower than with no modulation. Thus, surprisingly, the *addition* of harmonics to a background "masker" tone can improve the detectability of a separate tone pulse.

The secret of this odd phenomenon is that all the extra harmonics must vary synchronously with the 700-Hz component. If the modulations of the harmonics are varied randomly in time, so that the peaks and valleys do not coincide, the 14-dB gain at 100% modulation disappears almost completely. Comodulation appears to be the necessary condition for the substantial reduction in masking gained by adding harmonics to the masker. Similar effects were reported earlier for modulated noise bands (Hall et al., 1984).

Although there are other factors that influence this phenomenon, comodulation masking release should be understood primarily as clear evidence of the significant role of pattern recognition in the auditory process. It appears again that, as we have seen several times before, simultaneous sounds are better distinguished if they have features that make them seem to spring from different sources. Sounds that vary identically in time, such as comodulated harmonics, are interpreted by the auditory system as belonging together. The "signal" of a tone pulse cannot be distinguished from a single modulated tone of the same frequency, but stands out clearly against the background created by a group of comodulated harmonics.

The role of comodulation in hearing, for grouping and segregating sounds, can be seen as the analogue of a well-known phenomenon in vision, illustrated in Fig. 3.16, where a single irregular dash is much easier to see if the pattern of equidistant dashes is repeated. In both cases, the whole is greater than the sum of the parts.

THE BENEFIT OF LISTENING WITH TWO EARS

Up to now we have considered only cases of monaural perception. For the previous chapter, this omission can be defended by pointing to the fact that the contribution of binaural hearing of single sounds consists mainly in adding directional information about the sound source. Of course this is a remarkable achievement of the auditory system, but it seems to be of secondary importance with respect to the scope of this book. However, binaural perception is rather important for considering how simultaneous sounds undergo perceptual separation.

Binaural hearing has been studied primarily in terms of interaural time differences. We know that the auditory system can distinguish minimal horizontal differences in the direction of two frontal sound sources on the order of a few degrees, corresponding with a temporal difference of only about 20 sec (Blauert, 1983). This sensitivity to interaural time differences contributes to the detectability of a sound. For example, the detection threshold for a 1,000-Hz tone presented at the same time to both ears (frontal direction) can be lowered

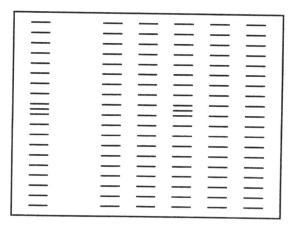

FIG. 3.16.   Demonstration that a single anomalous dash is much more easily distinguished in the context of a repeating regular dash pattern.

about 10 dB if the interaural time difference of a masking noise (lateral direction) is increased from zero to 0.6 msec.

"Head shadow" quantified in terms of interaural intensity differences can
also lead to improved audibility of sounds arriving from different directions.
The relative contributions of interaural time and level differences to the intelligibility of speech in the presence of a masking noise were studied by Bronkhorst
and Plomp (1988). The speech material, consisting of sentences read by a female speaker, was presented without interaural differences, and the noise, spectrally equal to the long-term average spectrum of the sentences, was varied as a
function of azimuth. Thus the testing condition mimicked the common situation of a speaker facing the listener, and an interfering noise coming from a different direction. In Fig. 3.17, the speech-reception threshold, defined as the
speech-to-noise ratio at which 50% of the sentences were correctly repeated by
the listeners, is plotted as a function of the azimuth. In these results, we see that
time differences alone can lower thresholds up to about 5 dB, level differences
alone up to about 8 dB, and the combined effects can lower thresholds by as
much as 10 dB.

Of course, these testing conditions represent a very favorable listening situation, where there is only a single disturbing noise source, without the complicat-
ing factor of sound reflections, which is the more typical case in everyday

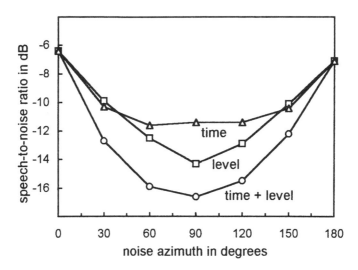

FIG. 3.17.   Mean speech-reception threshold for sentences presented in front of the listener as
a function of the direction of the noise source. The three curves represent the conditions where
only interaural time differences, only level differences due to head shadow, or both factors are
taken into account (redrawn from Bronkhorst & Plomp, 1988).

listening environments. The results demonstrate that, in addition to the effects discussed earlier in this chapter, binaural hearing can make a substantial contribution to the audibility and separation of simultaneous sounds. In chapter 5, some further comments on the relevance of this result are made within the framework of a general exposition regarding the intelligibility of fluent speech in the presence of disturbing noise.

DISCUSSION

The message of this chapter is that the auditory system is continuously testing whether simultaneous sounds originate from the same source or from different sources, and our surprising conclusion has been that this testing as well as the perceptual process of segregation into two or more sound streams is so successful that we are not consciously aware of this tremendous achievement. When an auditory signal is interrupted by louder sound bursts, the obliterated signal segments are heard as continuing straight through the interfering bursts. Successive tone pulses having a small frequency difference are perceived as parts of the same sound stream, whereas tone pulses with larger frequency differences are heard as multiple streams. The system seems to use all information available, that is, differences in timbre, pitch, and loudness, to decide which fragments belong together and should be perceived as such. Even absent speech fragments can be restored on the basis of contextual information.

The experimental evidence indicates that this process is controlled by a number of clear as well as flexible principles. The most significant one is the time scale of 75 to 200 msec for which the continuity and segregation effects are most prominent, and which corresponds to the duration of acoustic speech elements such as phonemes and syllables. Apparently, the time scale of the auditory–perceptual process on the one hand and the time scale of the acoustic units of our communication system on the other are very well matched.

Directly related to the previous point, it is remarkable that sequences of equal tones as visualized in Fig. 3.9 are not perceived as crossing each other. The auditory system's preference for grouping sounds of similar timbre on the basis of overall differences in pitch contributes to the perceptual separation of voices. However, this preference can be overruled by the criterion of similarity in timbre. Even a modest difference in timbre is sufficient for us to hear two sound streams as crossing each other, equally effective for separating simultaneous tone sequences or simultaneous voices.

This example illustrates that both pitch and timbre differences are "weighed" in the decision as to whether sound elements belong to the same stream or not, shown explicitly in Fig. 3.10. Timbre should be taken here in its widest sense, including spectrotemporal variations. For example, two complex tones where one is modulated in amplitude or frequency or begins slightly earlier than the other are much more easily separated than two tones that are more similar. As the comodulation effect illustrated in Figs. 3.14 and 3.15 showed, large timbre differences between signal and background can even improve detectability.

It is also interesting to note that longer sound sequences are more easily segregated than short ones. It is as if the auditory process allows the "benefit of the doubt" for a single pitch deviation but considers that repeated alternations reflect the presence of more than one sound stream. The fact that the temporal relations of (nonsimultaneous) segregated sound streams are difficult to perceive demonstrates that the auditory system directs all its efforts to separating the individual streams. Even the binaural hearing system is provided with sophisticated processes for improving the separation of sounds from different sources.

Without doubt, the most striking aspect of this unraveling process is the auditory system's capacity to restore inaudible sound fragments as if they were never masked. As illustrated in Fig. 3.5, even rhythmic properties are reconstructed with striking accuracy. These restorations in temporal structure are, however, much less stable than those observed for pitch and timbre. As we saw, training listeners on a particular time pattern can result in their hearing a correspondingly restored sound stream.

This restoration capability becomes particularly manifest in cases in which the system has only a small fragment of a sound to work with. Take, for example, the case of a single sinusoidal tone presented against a background of wide-band noise. If the tone is relatively weak, the auditory system does not exclude that the tone is the only audible harmonic of a low-pitched complex tone (illustrated in Fig. 3.18). In this case, context is used to decide upon the most likely reconstruction. This can explain why Houtgast's (1976) listeners were able to perceive a single weak tone as the harmonic of a lower fundamental and thus decide on its corresponding pitch. In his experiment, as well as in the earlier ones utilizing more harmonics, a necessary condition for hearing the tones as harmonics was a low sensation level as well as the presence of comparison tones having a similar timbre, which served to direct the listener's attention to the pitch range where the (inaudible) fundamental could be expected.

A related experiment was reported by Shriberg (1992). She presented her subjects with isolated vowels excised from natural speech. Low-pass filtering of these vowels resulted in frequent identification errors, which could be reduced significantly by adding high-pass filtered noise. Apparently, the noise

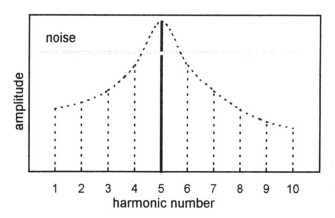

FIG. 3.18.   Illustration of the condition in which the ear cannot decide whether a single weak tone audible against a background of noise represents a single sinusoidal tone or the strongest harmonic of complex tone with a lower pitch.

improved the auditory system's ability to restore the high-frequency part of the vowel spectra.

Perceptual uncertainty regarding the original signal is maximal for fluent speech that is partially masked by other sounds. In this case the contribution of the context for retrieving any mutilated speech fragment is essential. As discussed in chapter 5, listeners report hearing quite different phonemes depending on context. This restoration can be so perfectly misleading that quite sophisticated processes must be involved.

Such results demonstrate even more convincingly than in the previous chapter that hearing represents an active process in which the incoming information is reorganized so as to derive the most probable reconstruction of the undisturbed sounds radiated from the various (predicted) sources. This reconstruction of auditory "objects" is so complete that moving our head does not destroy the stability of the acoustic world, no more than our eye movements perturb the world we see.

Our ability to segregate sounds may seem so obvious that we take it for granted. However, a simple demonstration of the effect can show how striking it can be. For example, if a fluent speech or music signal is alternated about three times per second with more intense wide-band noise, we hear the speech or music as *disturbed* by the noise bursts but still as a continuous signal. If the noise bursts are replaced with silent intervals, a completely different impression results: Now the speech or music is heard as a *mutilated* signal, an impression that immediately disappears if the noise is reintroduced. Apparently, silent intervals are perceived as belonging to the stimulus itself, whereas noise bursts are perceived as foreign sounds (i.e., produced by a different source). As we have seen, even intelligibility improves when the silent intervals are filled with noise.

With the phenomena discussed in the previous chapter, but still more with the discoveries reviewed in this chapter, we are far removed from the primitive picture of listening that was current half a century ago. The tacit supposition that a complete formulation of auditory psychophysics could be obtained by studying the perception of single sinusoidal tones has been replaced by the view that hearing is primarily typified by organizational characteristics. Single sounds "make sense" insofar as they are parts of a meaningful structure, and the system focuses all its efforts on finding this structure. This means that sounds are not accepted on their acoustic face value, as a mechanical sound analyzer would do, but are assumed to be a probable mixture of different messages from different sources, to be unraveled as effectively as possible. Audition is controlled by highly sophisticated principles, where the context of a sound element appears to be at least as important as the sound itself.

We have described this conclusion as the result of experimental evidence obtained with tones and noise bursts, which are still rather abstract stimuli. These insights are useful as a basis for exploring how speech is perceived, the topic of the next two chapters.

CONCLUSIONS

The previous chapter focused on spectral factors that contribute to the unique way in which tone complexes are analyzed, and this chapter considered temporal factors involved in sound analysis. We saw that the auditory system can process a mixture of multiple sound streams that are partially masking each other, as in a concert or a cocktail party, as if they were never superimposed. Not only are the mutually interfering sound fragments sorted according to their sources, but the inaudible parts are restored as convincingly as if they had never been masked. This remarkable achievement reveals that auditory processing is effectively designed for its everyday task of segregating, and identifying, the multiple sounds in our environment. The listener requires a reliable picture of the acoustic surround in order to react appropriately, and active perceptual processes are optimally adapted to deliver this information.

4
Speech Perception 1:
The Quest for Speech Units

We dealt in the previous chapters predominantly with rather simple stimuli such as tones and bursts of noise. These stimuli are easy to make and well suited to studying timbre, pitch, and loudness, as well as the perceptual segregation of sequences of tones into multiple sound streams. However, the more or less steady-state sound pulses of the laboratory are quite different from what we hear in everyday life, where most sounds vary continuously in time, and usually simultaneously in all three attributes of timbre, pitch, and loudness. It would be a serious mistake to think that with only these aspects of perception we have grasped the essential properties of the hearing process. On the contrary, they constitute merely a necessary introduction to the discussion of the real achievements of the system. Only a discussion of the way in which *dynamic* sounds are perceived can reveal what hearing really is.

Without doubt, the human voice is the most important sound we perceive. Roughly schematized, we use our eyes for spatial orientation and our ears for social communication. The blind may appear to be much more seriously handicapped than the deaf, but this is a superficial observation. We should realize that the mental development of a deaf child is strongly affected by the great barrier that hearing impairment presents to interhuman contacts. We might suppose that, intellectually, such strongly reduced linguistic accessibility can be largely compensated by reading, but this appears not to be true.

Speech communication is so important that it is rightly considered to be the most characteristic feature of the human race. Moreover, it has so many interesting aspects that I devote two chapters to it. As speech can be considered to be the stimulus with the most complex dynamic variation, it is, apart from its specific properties and function, a good prototype against which other sounds may be compared.

The study of speech as a dynamic signal could be initiated effectively only after equipment became available to study its parameters. Of course, in everyday speech perception, we are dealing with fluent speech. But just as we needed the previous chapters to prepare for entering the speech area, we have to consider first some basic aspects of the speech stimulus before we can move on to discussing the intelligibility of fluent speech in the next chapter. It may seem almost self-evident that vowels and consonants are the building blocks of perceived speech, just as are the letters in writing but, as demonstrated later, this apparent similarity is misleading. It is argued here that words are better candidates as the fundamental units of speech perception.

THE DREAM OF VISIBLE SPEECH

In the November 9, 1945, issue, *Science* announced the invention of a device, developed at Bell Telephone Laboratories during World War II, that would prove to revolutionize speech research: the sound spectrograph (Potter, 1945). This device made it possible for the first time to study effectively the dynamic aspects that are so essential to and characteristic of the speech signal. Although use of the spectrograph has been largely restricted to scientific research, its origin had to do with military interest in a device that would transpose the speech signal into a visual pattern that could be read by the eye. From Alexander Solzhenitsyn's autobiographical novel *The First Circle*, we know that the Soviet government was equally interested in "reading" speech spectrograms, in particular, for speaker identification. As a political prisoner working in a military laboratory, Solzhenitsyn was involved in a project to unmask an official as an "enemy of the people" because he had warned a friend by telephone about the friend's imminent arrest.

Essentially, the sound spectrograph is a very simple apparatus. It imitates the ear's frequency-analyzing power by splitting the speech signal by means of a series of band filters, usually 300 Hz wide, covering the frequency range up to 3,600 Hz. The output signals of the band filters were used to modulate the brightness of small electric lamps in front of a moving belt covered with phosphor, such that the phosphor emitted light for some time after having passed the lamps. Figure 4.1 gives an example of an early spectrogram.

At the time, it was assumed that there is a close correspondence between the letters of the written language and the vowels and consonants of the spoken language. As Jones wrote in a book on phonemes first published in 1950 (Jones, 1950/1976):

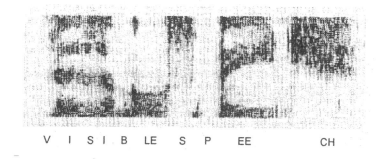

V   I   SI . B   LE   S   P   EE   CH

FIG. 4.1.   Spectrogram of the words "visible speech" (Potter, Kopp, & Green, 1947).

> When we speak, we think we utter successions of sounds most of which are held on for an
> appreciable time; and when we listen to speech, we think we hear similar successions of
> sounds. The effect is so definite to us that we have as a rule no particular difficulty in saying
> what the sounds in words are, or in assigning letters to them in alphabetic writing. (p. 2)

Hence, it is not surprising that the designers of the spectrograph expected appropriately trained persons to be able to identify visually what had been said.
Initial reports on use of the spectrograph indicated that trainees needed on the
average about a quarter of an hour to learn to "read" a new word, and that after
some additional training, they were able to converse satisfactorily among themselves (via spectrogram reading) as long as they talked clearly and at a fairly slow
rate. Although it was not said explicitly, we may assume that the training was restricted to words spoken in isolation.

As can be expected, the potential nonmilitary application of the spectrograph was its use as a speech-translation aid for the deaf. Two years after its first
announcement, a entire book on the sound spectrograph under the title *Visible
Speech* was published (Potter, Kopp, & Green, 1947). More than half of this
book was devoted to lessons on how to read spectrograms, indicating the great
expectations the authors had concerning the future of the spectrograph. As O.
E. Buckley, the president of Bell Telephone Laboratories, wrote in the foreword
(ignoring the device's military origin): "It was the hope of making the telephone
available to the totally deaf that the development of a mechanism for portraying
speech sounds visibly was undertaken" (p. XIII).

The final sentences of the book reveal the uninhibited optimism of the
originators:

> If and when it is found that deaf youngsters can learn to speak intelligibly and to read
> improved forms of visible speech with the same facility that they do their ABC's, and
> to do things with this form of writing that are practically impossible with the ABC's, it

will be time to consider seriously questions of more widespread use. What happens during the coming years in the field of deaf education can have a considerable effect upon the future of visible speech. If it comes into general use as a voice-written language for the deaf it could even start a trend toward modernized writing and printing. The deaf may lead the way! (pp. 421–422)

These enthusiastic words were written half a century ago. Such great expectations, however, have not been realized. A revised version of the spectrograph, with the moving belt of phosphor replaced by a drum with strips of recording paper, developed by Kay Instruments, has served as a major laboratory tool for some decades, but the original aim of the authors is almost forgotten. Reading spectrograms has proven to be much more difficult than originally described. For instance, it has been reported that a single (highly motivated) person needed training of more than a year, 2 hours a day, to read recordings of fluent speech that were still 20 times slower than real-time speech (Cole, Rudnicky, Zue, & Reddy, 1980). This disappointing result can explain why the spectrograph has never proven feasible as an aid for the deaf. (However, the spectrograph has enjoyed widespread use in speech therapy, to provide visual feedback comparing the speech productions of a client, whether one with hearing impairment or one with a speech/voice disorder, vs. the therapist's model.)

Why is it impossible to read spectrograms as quickly as we are able to read written text? This is the basic question we need to discuss in order to gain some insight into how speech is perceived.

THE PHONEMES AS LETTERS OF AN ALPHABET

As indicated earlier, the belief behind the development of the spectrograph was that spoken *phonemes*, vowels and consonants, would have a discrete nature corresponding with their alphabetic symbols. After having emphasized that an exact definition of the phoneme is not possible, Jones (1950/1976) explained the term as follows:

> A phoneme is a family of sounds in a given language which are related in character and are used in such a way that no one member ever occurs in a word in the same phonetic context as any other member. (p. 10)

Jones was speaking about defining phonemes in terms of "minimal pairs," which is a linguistic rather than an acoustic concept. Alphabetic symbols can be misleading cues to these types of distinctions. For instance, different languages may share the same graphemes (letters), but these may not represent exactly the same phonemes. Just as each written language consists of a fixed number of different letters, its spoken counterpart is considered to have an "alphabet" of basic sounds at its disposal, each of them expressible by a unique phonetic symbol. The discussion in this chapter reveals more about the ambiguous nature of the phoneme as applied to speech perception.

Let us begin by considering the consistency of the phoneme as a one-to-one correspondent of a specific acoustic segment of speech. Take, for example, the word /bæg/,[1] frequently used in the past to illustrate the dynamic character of the speech signal. Thinking in terms of the correspondence between spoken and written language, one assumes that the speaker wants to pronounce the successive phonemes /b/, /æ/, and /g/ but, due to the physical restrictions of the vocal tract, the corresponding shapes and movements do not follow each other discretely in time but are combined into an almost unanalyzable single ballistic gesture. Liberman (1970) illustrated (see Fig. 4.2) how the acoustic signal of the word changes continuously in time and cannot be split up into three discrete segments representing the /b/, /æ/, and /g/. In this combination, none of the phonemes is represented as it should "ideally" be. The vocal-tract gestures connected with each phoneme seem to overlap, an effect for which the term *coarticulation* was coined. Consequently, the hearing system of the listener is presented with the difficult task of recovering from the coarticulated signal the three phonemes the speaker had in mind, corresponding with the three letters of the written version of the same word.

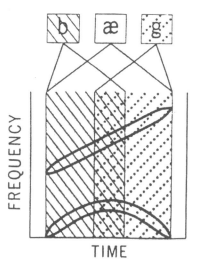

FIG. 4.2. A schematic representation of the coarticulation of successive phonemes (Liberman, 1970).

---

[1]In agreement with general use, phonetic symbols are marked by slashes.

The problem of reconstructing alphabetic (phonemic) equivalents from the heavily coarticulated speech signal was perhaps never more better expressed than by Hockett in 1955:

> Imagine a row of Easter eggs carried along a moving belt; the eggs are of various sizes and variously colored, but not boiled. At a certain point, the belt carries the row of eggs between two rollers of a wringer, which quite effectively smash them and rub them more or less into each other. The flow of eggs before the wringer represents the series of impulses from the phoneme source; the mess that emerges from the wringer represents the output of the speech transmitter. At a subsequent point, we have an inspector whose task it is to examine the passing mess and decide, on the basis of the broken and unbroken yolks, the variously spread-out albumen, and the variously colored bits of shell, the nature of the flow of eggs which previously arrived at the wringer. Notice that he does not have to try to put the eggs together again—a manifest physical impossibility—but only to identify. (p. 210)

How?

> What a native listener does, therefore, to the signal which comes to his ear, is ultimately equivalent to redistributing the sound-qualities along the time-scale, putting some part of the vowel-quality into the preceding consonantal segment [Hockett referred to the word *back*, RP] and some in the following one, so that each is perceived as being what it must be even if the consonantal phase (acoustically defined) is inaudible, and leaving the residue (after those abstractions) to be heard as the correct vowel phoneme. (p. 210)

This view was expressed again, essentially unaltered, 20 years later (Liberman, Shankweiler, Fischer, & Carter, 1974) as follows:

> To recover the phonemes from the sound into which they are so complexly encoded requires a decoder which segments the continuous acoustic signal according to linguistic rules. Though we cannot guess how such a decoder might work, we know that it functions quite automatically for all speaker-hearers of a language, even very young children. (p. 204)

This in fact has been the prevailing concept up to the present. Forty years after the spectrogram had confronted the investigators with the problem, Nittrouer and Studdert-Kennedy (1987) admitted:

> We still have ... no firm understanding of the function of coarticulation (if any) in listening. Is coarticulation necessary and intrinsic to production, and must a listener therefore draw on the contextually variable information that it carries to recover the phonetic message? Or is coarticulation simply a result of a speaker becoming rapid and skillful? If so, are the acoustic consequences of coarticulation merely noise that a listener filters out? (p. 319)

It is clear from these quotations that the authors all consider that phonemes are the building blocks of speech sounds, and that accurate, segmented identification of phonemes is the basis of speech perception. However, it is also clear that these authors found the identification of phonemes, in view of the phenomenon of coarticulation, a rather enigmatic process. For some authors, this difficulty has been met by assuming that, in view of the acoustic variability of the speech signal (considered in the next chapter), the perception of phonemes must be closely related to their *production*.

This reasoning seems to be inevitable if one accepts that, just as written language is governed by an alphabet of letters, spoken language is governed by an alphabet of phonemes. Perhaps Joos (1948) was the first to explain the invariance of the perceived phonemes in terms of their production. A few years later, Licklider (1952) was still more explicit, concluding:

> It is possible that the process of identification operates on the *motor form* [italics added, RP] of the signal rather than upon the sensory form. Or, more probably, the process involves both the sensory and the motor patterns. (p. 594)

A. M. Liberman at Haskins Laboratories was the first speech scientist who developed this approach most fully, in what has become known as the *motor theory of speech perception*. In its original version, developed in the 1950s, the theory concluded that speech perception is based on recovering the motor commands involved in phonemic production as, for example, lip rounding and jaw raising (Liberman, 1957; Liberman, Cooper, Shankweiler, & Studdert-Kennedy, 1967). Further evidence regarding the "mutilation" of coarticulation, and the great variation of motor gestures, has more recently led these authors (cf. Liberman & Mattingly, 1985) to suggest that it is not the actual gestures, but the *intended* gestures associated with the individual phonemes, that are the identification targets. Thus the *variant* execution (varying in both motor detail and acoustic result) is considered to stand for the *invariant* intention.

As the phoneme was almost universally accepted as the building block of speech, not only in terms of production but also for perception, it is no wonder that the motor theory was accepted by many speech scientists, particularly in the beginning. The impact of the theory was fortified by experimental evidence considered to support it. For example, an early experiment carried out by Liberman, Delattre, and Cooper (1952) examined the degree to which the identification of the initial stop consonants /p/, /t/, and /k/ depends on the following vowel. Twelve synthetic stops (consisting of short noise bursts) with energy concentrated in different frequency bands varying in steps of 360 Hz were each combined with seven different vowels. Figure 4.3 represents schematically

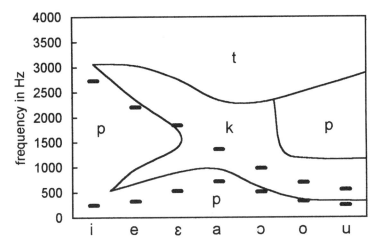

FIG. 4.3.   Areas indicating the energy concentration of synthetic initial stop consonants predominantly identified as /p/, /t/, or /k/. The horizontal dashes indicate the formant frequencies
of the seven vowel sounds tested (based on data from Liberman, Delattre, & Cooper, 1952).

the areas over which listeners identified the stops predominantly as /p/, /t/, or
/k/. Apparently, the perceptual salience of (expected) coarticulation is so great
that, for example, a noise burst centered at about 1,500 Hz is heard as /p/ before
some vowels but /k/ before others. The authors concluded that the acoustic
properties of a phoneme (by which they meant the noise burst, not the noise
burst in context) are unreliable as a clue for its identification.

Another frequently used argument for the motor (as opposed to an auditory)
theory of speech perception was the fact that speech can be followed at rates as
high as 30 phonemes per second, much more rapidly than if the speech signal
were a string of temporally independent (noncoarticulated) acoustic events. As
we saw in the previous chapter, a random sequence of different speech sounds
presented at that rate is heard as a disordered and confused mass of sounds,
quite different from the clear and comprehensible signal that is the way speech
appears to a practiced listener. However, we also found that this perceptual phenomenon is not unique to speech and that it depends on the difference between
sudden versus gradual transitions in timbre and pitch.

A remarkable phenomenon, first described by Liberman, Harris, Hoffman,
and Griffith in 1957, was considered to provide strong support for the motor
theory. With the help of hand-painted spectrograms, these researchers were
able to generate speechlike sounds varying in small steps between pairs of consonants. For example, the voiced stop consonants /b/, /d/, and /g/, followed by
the vowel /e/ (as in *gate*), differ in the direction and extent of the sec-

ond-formant transition. The authors created a b-d-g continuum by varying this parameter in 14 equal steps covering the entire range. When these stimuli were presented to listeners under a forced-choice identification task, with responses restricted to /b/, /d/, or /g/, the authors reported that most listeners tended to divide the continuum into three sharply defined phoneme categories, with very abrupt labeling transitions. In a subsequent same–different discrimination task using pairs of the same stimuli, the authors reported that pairs were much better discriminated if they straddled a phoneme boundary than if they came from within a phoneme's range.

The authors concluded that the listeners had based their decisions primarily on an abstract notion of phoneme category rather than on the actual acoustic differences, as one might have predicted on psychophysical grounds. This phenomenon, which came to be known as *categorical perception*, was put forward as strong evidence that "speech is special," that is, that speech is not processed according to the same perceptual laws as other types of sounds. This in fact became more and more the main (and almost exclusive) argument in favor of the motor theory of perception, initiating hundreds of publications pro and con, including an entire volume devoted to the topic (Harnad, 1987). The primary question in this controversy became whether categorical perception was unique to speech or was actually a basic property of the perceptual process in general, but manifesting itself primarily for highly familiar sounds.

As pointed out by Lane (1965) in an early critical review, Liberman et al. (1957) used in their description (see the summary given earlier) the mitigating expressions *most listeners* and *tended to divide*, indicating that the effect was not as rigid as one would like, to support the invocation of a special mode of speech perception, different in kind from the perception of all other types of stimuli.[2] As more recent experimental evidence (e.g., human perception of musical sounds and animal perception of speech sounds) has accumulated, the phenomenon of categorical perception has come to be seen as much more complex and much more universal, and thus has lost its original theoretical significance. Therefore, a further discussion of categorical perception is postponed to chapter 6. Of course, the dubious theoretical significance of categorical perception does not entirely undercut the motor theory itself.

Scientists not happy with the motor theory searched assiduously for qualities of the *pronounced* rather than the *intended* phoneme that might explain its identification. I restrict myself here to some experiments by Stevens and Blumstein,

---

[2]For an extensive discussion of the merits of the motor theory of speech perception, see Mattingly and Studdert-Kennedy (1991).

who made the most extensive investigations. As with the studies at the Haskins Laboratories, these experiments were almost exclusively focused on stop consonants, particularly the auditory differentiation of /b/, /d/, and /g/.

In an initial series of experiments, Stevens and Blumstein (1978) considered whether the identification of the consonants in synthetic consonant–vowel syllables with different vowels can be explained by acoustic attributes of the stimuli. They found that, independent of the vowel, the gross shape of the spectrum sampled at the consonantal release has a distinctive form for each place of articulation: a diffuse-falling spectrum for /b/, a diffuse-rising spectrum for /d/, and a prominent midfrequency spectral peak for /g/. The scores of about 80% of the listeners could be explained by these spectral differences. In a subsequent study using real speech (Blumstein & Stevens, 1979) the unvoiced stop consonants /p/, /t/, and /k/ were also included. The spectra of the onsets of consonant–vowel syllables and the offsets of vowel–consonant syllables were matched to templates based on the three spectral shapes referred to above. About 85% of the analyzed spectra were correctly classified by using the templates. A third study (Blumstein & Stevens, 1980) showed that segments as short as 10 to 20 msec sampled from the onset of real consonant–vowel syllables are sufficient for listeners to identify the three voiced stop consonants, and in most cases the vowel as well.

The authors offered these results as positive evidence that the stop consonants can be identified on the basis of invariant spectral differences. However, we should realize that the moderate scores of 80–85% were obtained for isolated syllables. As demonstrated in chapter 5 for vowels, we can expect that the identification of stop consonants in free conversation is considerably more difficult than for syllables pronounced in the laboratory. Apparently, Blumstein and Stevens (1980), too, were not entirely easy about their speculations regarding invariant cues. They wrote:

> When the spectrum at onset does not provide clear-cut information about place of articulation, listeners resort to other, secondary, cues based on formant motions. Rising trajectories of formants 2 and 3 tend to provide [b] responses, falling transitions [d] responses, and spreading formants [g] responses. (p. 658)

Walley and Carrell (1983) verified this supposed order of onset cues and transition cues by creating stimuli for which the onset spectra conflicted with the formant transitions. They found, however, that listeners' responses, whether from adults or children, were generally determined by the formant transitions.

Thus we may conclude that even very sophisticated attempts to identify invariant properties of stop consonants have not yielded convincing results.

Short-term spectra that are independent of the following vowel are not sufficient for consistent consonant identification. The experiments did not provide clear evidence against the motor theory of speech perception.

COARTICULATION: A NATURAL RATHER THAN A DISTURBING PHENOMENON

The previous section made clear that coarticulation, understood as the mutual interaction of successively *pronounced* phonemes, has typically been considered only as a distortion of *intended* phonemes. Yet, if coarticulation "disturbs" phonemes, one should then expect that isolated phonemes are more readily identified than are phonemes in running speech.

That coarticulation may actually help rather than hinder phonemic identification was dramatically demonstrated soon after the introduction of the spectrograph by Harris (1953). He found, for example, that if he edited the /d/ from the real word /dik/ and put it together with the /æk/ from /kæk/, creating the new word /dæk/, the initial consonant in the newly synthesized word not only sounded unnatural, but was essentially unintelligible. He concluded:

> To synthesize speech with reasonable naturalness, the influence factor should be included. Here these influences can be approximated by employing more than one building block to represent each linguistic element and by selecting these blocks properly, taking into account the spectral characteristics of adjacent sounds so as to approximate the time pattern of the formant structure occurring in ordinary speech. (p. 962)

Harris's work, carried out at Bell Telephone Laboratories in cooperation with its director R. K. Potter, offered one explanation as to why spectrograms were so difficult to read. The "influence factor," Harris's term for coarticulation, indicated how tightly coupled successive phonemes are with regard to their perception. Although these experiments showed that the perception of consonants is strongly dependent on coarticulation with neighboring vowels, the findings did not address the question of whether the phenomenon as such should be evaluated as a "positive" or "negative" factor in speech perception.

The role of coarticulation has been investigated extensively for the vowels. For example, if coarticulation impeded the identification of phonemes (had a "negative" effect), one would expect that vowel identification would be more accurate for sustained vowels as opposed to vowels coarticulated with consonants. Strange, Verbrugge, Shankweiler, and Edman (1976) tested this hypothesis by comparing listeners' accuracy in identifying isolated vowels versus vowels pronounced in syllables such as /pip/, /pIp/, and so on. The result was the opposite of the "negative" effect prediction: 69% of the isolated vowels were correctly identified, as opposed to 91% of the syllabic-nucleus vowels. These scores were obtained for vowels pronounced by the same speaker. Mixing the utterances of different speakers resulted in lower scores of 57% and 83%, respectively, but confirmed the same finding—that interactions with neighboring consonants can contribute in a positive way to vowel identification.

This unexpected finding initiated a number of investigations in which the contributions of initial and final consonants to vowel identity were studied in more detail. For example, Strange and Bohn (1998) tested 14 different German vowels as pronounced in the syllable /d(vowel)t/. German was chosen for this experiment because the formant frequencies of its vowels are much more consistent than in American English (i.e., they form much better monophthongs). Possible additional advantages include the number of vowels, and the fact that they were pronounced in the context of the carrier sentence *Ich habe /d(vowel)t/ gesagt* (*I said /d(vowel)t/*). Each individual target word was pronounced twice by the same German speaker, and each of these tokens was then split into three parts representing the initial consonant, the vowel center, and the final consonant (roughly 25%, 50%, and 25%, respectively, of the original word's duration). These edited fragments were then presented to different groups of German listeners, who were asked to match each presented fragment against a list of target words printed in standard German orthography. Their average correct scores, ordered from lowest to highest, are plotted in Fig. 4.4.

As indicated in the figure, the lowest scores were obtained when only the initial or the final 25% of the word was presented. When segments of the central, steady-state portion of the vowels were presented (all vowels adjusted to the same duration), only 53% of the original words were correctly identified. A much higher score (70%) was obtained when the initial and final 25% "consonant" portions were presented together, separated by a silent center adjusted to such a length that the total "word" durations were the same for all stimuli.

Note that in these conditions exclusively spectral information was presented, whereas the other three conditions also contained information about the duration of the spoken vowel. The first was the vowel center, with its actual duration maintained. The score of 85% is indeed much higher than when duration information is lacking but, surprisingly, still lower than the score of 90% obtained for the initial and final consonants where the syllable center was replaced by a silent interval.

These results clearly demonstrate that syllable fragments, even when edited to represent only consonants, contain substantial information about neighboring vowels. The fact that medial vowel segments when presented

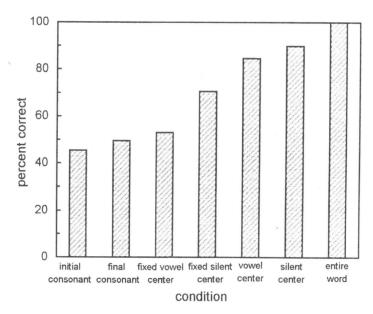

FIG. 4.4.   Percentage of correctly identified vowels with only the indicated parts of the word /d(vowel)t/ presented to the listeners (based on data from Strange & Bohn, 1998).

alone led to relatively low vowel-identification scores does not support the view, held by most speech scientists in the past, that sustained vowels are the ideal form of a vowel, imperfectly realized in actual speech. In fact, Strange (1989) proposed an alternative theory, that the articulatory specification of a vowel is not only determined by a specific spectral target but also by a characteristic temporal movement pattern of the vocal tract. That is, the vowel gesture is still specified independently of the preceding and following consonant gestures but, due to the considerable temporal overlap of vowel and consonant movements, the formant trajectories are a joint function of both consonant and vowel gestures. Thus Strange's explanation is still very much couched in the terms of the motor theory of speech perception.

The conclusion that coarticulation contributes to vowel identification does not automatically mean that this is also true for consonants. Nittrouer and Studdert-Kennedy (1987) created a synthetic /ʃ/–/s/ continuum followed by one of four natural vocalic portions: /i/ and /u/ produced with transitions appropriate for either /ʃ/ or /s/. For listeners, they recruited adults and also children between the ages of 3 and 7 years. Results of the testing indicated that perceptual sensitivity to certain forms of coarticulation seems to be present from a very early age, and the authors concluded that it may therefore be intrinsic to the process of speech perception.

A quite different approach was followed by Diehl and coauthors (Diehl, Kluender, Foss, Parker, & Gernsbacher, 1987). They synthesized randomized lists of /b(vowel)s/, /d(vowel)s/, and /g(vowel)s/ syllables, utilizing 10 different vowels, and presented them to three groups of listeners. The first group were instructed to push a button immediately upon recognizing the initial consonant /b/, the second group responded to /d/, and the third were given /g/ as a target. Results indicated that reaction time (RT) correlated positively with the duration of the following vowel (i.e., RTs were longer when the vowel was longer). The authors interpreted this as suggesting that "consonant recognition is vowel dependent" and, more specifically, that "a certain amount or proportion of the vowel formant trajectory must be evaluated before consonants can be reliably identified" (p. 570). Again, coarticulation appeared to be contributing in a positive way to identification.

In a later study, van Son and Pols (1995) investigated whether the contribution of coarticulation to identification is restricted to the influence of immediately neighboring phonemes or extends over a larger range. In contrast to the studies already discussed, these authors used fragments taken from a longer, read text rather than isolated words. In addition, they tested a large number of different consonants and vowels. The results provided strong evidence that the identification of both vowels and consonants can be improved by acoustic information from beyond the boundaries of the transitions to neighboring phonemes. It was found that information from the speech ahead of the target segment improved identification more than information from speech after the segment, even when the transition boundaries were exceeded.

Finally, it is important to recognize the role of silent gaps in phoneme identification. For example, Best, Morrongiello, and Robson (1981) observed that hearing *say* or *stay* depends on the duration of the silent gap (preceding the /t/) in the word, indicating the significance of the overall dynamical structure in distinguishing /s/ from /st/.

We may conclude on the basis of the evidence presented in this section that coarticulation should be seen as a natural and contributing rather than a disturbing phenomenon. It is clear that the apparently strong intermingling of spectral as well as temporal features of neighboring phonemes makes it more and more difficult to insist that discrete phonemes are the basic units of speech perception. I return to this question at the end of this chapter, after addressing some quite different approaches to the phoneme problem.

HOW INFANTS LEARN TO SPEAK

Over the last 20 years much research has been conducted regarding the development of speech understanding and speech production by infants.[3] These studies have shed surprising new light on how speech is perceived in general. Perhaps the best way to summarize the main results is by distinguishing the stages ordered according to their developmental chronology.

1. *Discrimination of speech sounds.* Eimas, Siqueland, Jusczyk, & Vigorito (1971) showed that infants as young as 1 month of age not only are responsive to speech sounds, but also are able to discriminate fine differences in speech, for example, /p/ versus /b/. This ability can be measured by observing an increase in conditioned response rate to a second, novel speech sound following habituation to an initial speech sound. The infant's discriminative ability appears to be independent of whether or not the difference tested is actually used in the language heard by the child. Experiments with nonspeech sounds suggest that this capacity is not restricted to speech—apparently, infants come supplied with a general, language-independent capacity to discriminate the types of acoustic contrasts used in speech.

However, as development proceeds, a selection seems to take place. Although American infants at the age of 6 to 8 months can still discriminate non-English contrasts, only a fraction of them can do so at 8 to 10 months, and hardly any at 10–12 months (Jusczyk, Friederici, Wessels, Svenkerud, & Jusczyk, 1993; Jusczyk, Houston, & Goodman, 1998). Several investigations have shown that this decline in the ability to react to nonnative contrasts takes place during the period of 6 to 12 months of age. Although this has been interpreted mostly as a decline in sensitivity, it may be more likely a decline in *attention*: Sound contrasts not heard in the child's native language fail to capture the infant's interest. This has been found not only for consonants, but also for vowels, and even for whole words. The hearing process seems to be preparing itself to focus on just those differences that will be relevant to the child in learning language.

2. *Comprehension of words.* This type of selective attention occurring at the age of 6 to 12 months may be seen as related to the first signs of the child's comprehension of words, generally considered as beginning in the period between 8 and 10 months. Hallé and de Boysson-Bardies (1994) examined whether 11- and 12-month-old infants can distinguish familiar versus unfamiliar words in a situation yielding no extralinguistic cues. Head-turn preference was used as a

---

[3]For general reviews, see Bloom (1993), Jusczyk (1995), and Kuhl (1987).

criterion. Results indicated that the infants turned and looked significantly longer in the direction of the loudspeaker when familiar words were presented. The difference in looking time for familiar versus rare words pointed to a rapid development of this capacity around the age of 11 months. Other tests reported by Jusczyk and Aslin (1995) suggest that some ability to detect familiar words in fluent speech contexts may be present by as early as 7½ months of age. This development reflects the infant's growing interest in objects, persons, and events in the surrounding world.

3. *Production of babble.* In the meantime, a comparable selection process has started with respect to the sounds the infant is producing. At about 6 months the child begins to babble strings of alternating consonants and vowels, such as *babababa*. The stimulating role of intact hearing in the development of such vocalization is convincingly indicated by the observation that babbling in deaf infants is delayed by at least 6 months (Oller & Eilers, 1988). For hearing children, in the period up to 12 months of age, babbling sounds become more and more tuned to the speech sounds heard by the child. An extensive longitudinal study of sounds produced by infants from four different language backgrounds (de Boysson-Bardies, Hallé, Sagart, & Durand, 1989) showed that vowels gradually become more and more like those the child hears in the respective languages. A similar development has been noted for consonants.

4. *Production of words.* In this way the infant is prepared to produce its first words at the age of 12 to 14 months (Benedict, 1979). By this time, the child's interest in the surrounding world has arrived at a level such that thoughts and feelings are directed to specific objects, persons as well as material things, and the child has discovered that spoken sounds seem to have specific meanings. This is an amazing development. The infant hears speech as a continuous stream and has to find out that certain segments have special significance. There is a growing awareness of regularity and order in the sounds heard, and the child finds that imitating these sounds appears to be effective in obtaining specific goals, such as food or toys. The child begins to comprehend that words stand for objects and actions.

By means of an expanding vocabulary, the child acquires more and more communicative control over its surroundings. Carey (1978) observed that, on average, infants produce their first words at the age of 14 months, with a progressive vocabulary increase at 19 months, and simple sentences begin to appear at 24 months. In the meantime, the child has learned to distinguish conceptually between things likely to have an individual name (e.g., a doll) and things not likely to have one (e.g., a box), indeed a remarkable achievement (Katz, Baker, & Macnamara, 1974). Carey estimated that by the age of 6, the average child has a lexicon of about 14,000 words, corresponding with learning on average nine new words per day.

It is interesting also to consider how the composition of words used by the young child appears to develop. The first words uttered by infants consist of simple syllables with single initial and final consonants (e.g., Ingram, 1974; Menn, 1978). Consonant clusters are apparently much more difficult to pronounce, and seem to be acquired as *routines* rather than as sequences of earlier learned individual phonemes. That special training is needed to pronounce unfamiliar consonant clusters is well known to adults learning a second language. The Dutch theoretical physicist M. J. G. Veltman mentioned in an interview after being awarded with the 1999 Nobel prize in physics that he gave his computer program the name *schoonschip* (/sxo:nsxɪp/) because foreigners are unable to pronounce the Dutch consonant combination /sx/.

5. *Learning of grammar.* As more words are learned, the child demonstrates a growing insight regarding how words are combined into sentences and other rules of the language. By 3 to 3.5 years of age, most children have mastered the basic morphological and syntactic structures of their language. They know how to combine words into meaningful sentences, and how meaning depends on the words selected as well as their order. In other words: The child has learned how to use words as building blocks for speech.[4]

The relative timing and process of growth in word comprehension (stage 2), word production (stage 4), and learning of grammar (stage 5) are visualized in Fig. 4.5, based on data from a longitudinal study by Goodman (Bates & Goodman, 1997). The curves agree very well with the findings reported by Benedict (1979) and Carey (1978) referred to earlier.

All experimental evidence just summarized supports the view that the young child is not aware of the existence of phonemes. The child learns to pronounce words consisting of phonemes, but without any indication of having discovered that, for example, the words *pit, top,* and *price* share the same /p/. It might be expected that, after having mastered to pronounce a word with a /p/, the child will start to pronounce other words with /p/ correctly, but this does not seem to be the case (Ferguson & Farwell, 1975). Words rather than phonemes appear to be the units of early production. For the child, the goal of language acquisition is *communication,* and it is always amazing to hear how a child's pronunciation mirrors the accent of the child's parents. I may refer to St. Augustine's vivid recollection of how he learned to speak (Harris, 1980):

---

[4]A recent review of the development of language acquisition is given by Clark (1995).

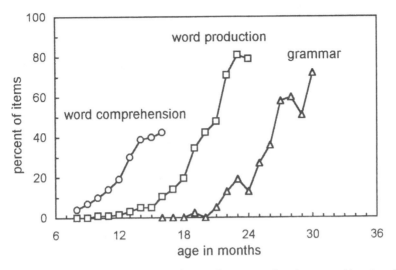

FIG. 4.5.   Median growth scores for word comprehension, word production, and learning of grammar by infants as a function of age (redrawn from Bates & Goodman, 1997).

When they (my elders) named some object, and accordingly moved towards something, I saw this and I grasped that the thing was called by the sound they uttered when they meant to point it out. Their intention was shown by their bodily movements, as it were the natural language of all peoples: the expression of the face, the play of the eyes, the movement of other parts of the body, and the tone of voice which expresses our state of mind in seeking, having, rejecting or avoiding something. Thus, as I heard words repeatedly used in their proper places in various sentences, I gradually learned to understand what objects they signified; and after I had trained my mouth to form these signs, I used them to express my own desires. (p. 41)

HOW CHILDREN LEARN TO READ

The question of whether or not young children are aware of the existence of phonemes as units of speech has been studied extensively in relation to how children learn to read. It is obvious that awareness of the existence of phonemes as the "alphabet" of spoken language—what has come to be known as *phonemic awareness*—would be of enormous help in learning to use comparable elements in reading. The nature and degree of such awareness in children have been studied in several ways. Some studies, representing quite different approaches, are discussed here.

Bruce (1964) designed an experiment in which no reading was required. In total, 67 children, representing five mental age groups between 5 and 10 years, were presented orally with 30 words appropriate for their age. For each spoken word, the child's task was to pronounce the real word that remained if a particular letter sound were to be taken away from the original word. For 10 test words, the sound removed was at the beginning, for another 10 a medial sound was omitted, and for 10 a final sound was removed. The residual words were always familiar words. Examples of words manipulated in this way, with the eliminated phoneme in parentheses, are: *(n)ice, ha(n)d, star(t)*. The children were trained for the task by being asked to: (a) say a word, (b) make a sound, (c) indicate first, middle, and last of a group in a picture, (d) repeat the first, middle, and last of three digits spoken by the experimenter, (e) demonstrate which, and how many, bricks are left when others have been separated from them by the subject, and (f) observe modeling of several examples of the experimental task.

Figure 4.6 shows the mean correct scores, with their standard deviations, for the five age groups. It is clear that the children represented a wide range in the ability to analyze spoken words into phonemes. As the chronological ages of the children varied from 5.1 to 7.5 years, it seems possible that the results were partly, or perhaps fully, determined by differences in reading experience.

The effect of learning to read was investigated some years later more explicitly in an experiment by Liberman et al. (1974). The test group included 46 preschool children (mean age 4.9 years), 49 kindergarten children (mean age 5.8 years), and 40 first-grade children (mean age 6.9 years). Under the guise of a "tapping game," half of the children were required to repeat a word or sound

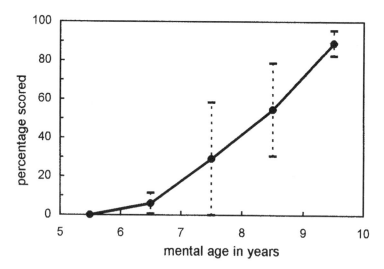

FIG. 4.6.   Mean score and standard deviation of residual words, correctly pronounced by children as a function of mental age, if a particular letter sound of the words was taken away (based on data from Bruce, 1964).

spoken by the examiner and to indicate, by tapping a small wooden dowel on the table, the number of phonemes, whereas the other half indicated the number of syllables. Test items varied from single vowels to three-phoneme words for the first subgroup and words of one to three syllables for the second subgroup. Figure 4.7 shows the percentage of children who, after some training, were able to tap correctly the number of phonemes or syllables in six consecutive items. These data suggest there is a dramatic increase in phoneme segmentation abilities from 0% of the preschoolers to 70% of children at the end of the first grade. Although preschool and kindergarten children are much better at identifying the number of syllables, these scores, too, improve with age, perhaps assisted by learning to read.

A quite different approach was used by Byrne and Fielding-Barnsley (1989). They taught preliterate children to read the written equivalent of spoken words such as *mat* and *sat*; subsequently they presented a written word *mow* and asked the child to judge whether it stood for the pronounced word *mow* or *sow*. From the poor results, the authors concluded that both phonemic awareness and grapheme–phoneme knowledge are needed to perform this task successfully. The experiment suggests that the ability to recognize the initial consonants of *mat* and *mow* as the "same" is not at all as "automatic" or self-evident as we

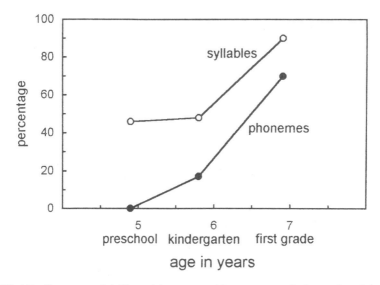

FIG. 4.7. Percentage of children of three groups able to tap correctly the number of phonemes or syllables of spoken words, as a function of their mean age (based on data from Liberman et al., 1974).

might think, but should be understood as an achievement related to the acquisition of alphabetic reading.

These studies demonstrate clearly, as is now generally accepted, that young children learn to speak without any previous notion that words consist of phonemes. The studies indicate, too, not only that the awareness of phonemes coincides chronologically with learning the alphabet but that the two are highly correlated. However, this correlation is no proof that phonemic awareness is *induced* by learning the alphabet—phonemic awareness may represent a typical stage in language acquisition that develops with age.

This question has been addressed by investigations in which adult nonreaders were presented with phoneme discrimination tasks. For example, Morais, Cary, Alegria, and Bertelson (1979) compared illiterate and literate adults in rural Portugal, and Read, Yun-fei, Hong-yin, and Bao-qing (1986) tested Chinese adults who had learned only Chinese characters versus others who had also learned *Hanyu pinyin* (writing Chinese words with alphabetic letters). In both experiments the subjects were requested to add individual consonants to, or delete them from, spoken real words as well as nonwords. The authors found that only subjects who had learned the alphabetic writing system in school could perform this task rather consistently (mean scores presented in Fig. 4.8). The fact that

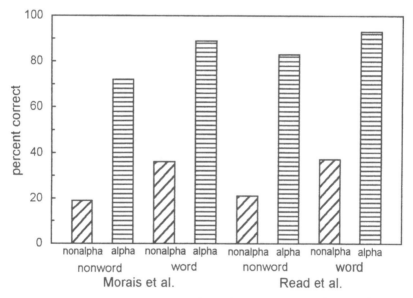

FIG. 4.8.   Percentage of adults unfamiliar ("nonalpha") and familiar ("alpha") with the written alphabet who were able to add or delete individual consonants from spoken words (based on data from Morais et al., 1979, in Portugal, and Read et al., 1986, in China).

some subjects defined as illiterates were partially successful might be due to the nature of the instructions or previous experience.

Further evidence that phonemic awareness may not emerge spontaneously but is the result of learning to read and write is indicated by the relative effectiveness of training procedures. The fact that accomplished readers seem to read words rather than strings of letters has led to the view that phoneme–grapheme correspondences need not be taught explicitly but will be discovered more or less automatically by the child in the process of learning how words are written.[5] However, this has not proven to be the most effective procedure. More explicit attention to the one-to-one relation between phonemes and letters (at least as a first-order approximation) seems to be a crucial factor in teaching children to read (for a discussion, see Morais & Kolinsky, 1995).

It is also significant that many children who show no problems learning to talk appear to have considerable difficulties learning to read (Liberman et al., 1974). Such children (and adults) may be able to learn that the written *b* stands for the sound /b/, *a* for /æ/, and *t* for /t/, but cannot sound out the written word *bat*. On the other hand, they may be able to learn that this word as a whole is a visual symbol of the spoken word /bæt/. The number of such individuals may in fact be quite large, as much as 30–40% of the population (Lauter, 1999; Lindamood, Bell, & Lindamood, 1997). Many of these individuals may compensate for their natural inability to hear out speech sounds inside syllables by an advanced proficiency for visually memorizing words like pictures, matched to spoken equivalents.

Thus beginning readers may read in a very different way than skilled readers (Gough, Juel, & Griffith, 1992). All children may begin by seeing printed words as pictographs representing spoken words comparable with pictures in a rebus. If a language consisted of only a small number of different words, this would be a sufficient strategy. However, the difficulties of differentiating written words on the basis of their overall appearance increase dramatically as the number of words increases. Moreover, this strategy provides no means of connecting new printed words with their spoken equivalents. Hence, it is necessary to learn the letter–phoneme correspondences in order to acquire an expanding reading vocabulary. Happily, most children seem to have no problems in learning this.

Of course, such a strategy is useful only in so far as the phoneme–grapheme correspondence of a language provides a reliable guide—a quality that differs markedly from language to language. Finnish and Spanish are languages with a

---

[5]For an extensive review of this question, see Chall (1967).

close correspondence, whereas French and particularly English[6] are much less consistent (Downing, 1973). For instance, children have to learn that the "same" vowel in English may be spelled in different ways, as in *out* and *crowd,* and that in other cases letters appear that are not pronounced, as in *know* and *doubt.*

Alphabetic representation of speech may be misleading with regard to the "natural" way that speech is represented internally. As Treiman and Baron (1981) said:

> A second possible explanation, one that we have proposed here, is that young children do not represent speech in terms of segments, either consciously or unconsciously. Rather, they represent the sound of a word or syllable "integrally," as an indivisible whole. This possibility is consistent with children's ability to hear and speak, and with their ability to judge that certain pairs of words sound different and that others are more alike. The fact that a child can do these things implies that he has *some* internal representation of speech—it does not tell what kind of representation. The possibility that young children represent spoken words wholistically is consistent with their apparent difficulties in hearing or repeating novel words (particularly those that are unlike any familiar words), and with their difficulties in telling *how* words sound alike or different. (p. 192)

In order to decide whether this explanation is right, we need to know more about the relation between speech and the alphabet. Traditionally, we are inclined to consider the written letters as derived from the spoken phonemes, but is this all that can be said? Is it too bold to suppose that, conversely, the very concept of the phoneme is based, at least in part, on our familiarity with graphemes? A study of the origins of our alphabet may help us obtain better insight into this question. Taking this historical journey may show us that the relation between written and spoken "alphabets" is much more complex than we thought.

THE ALPHABET AS A UNIQUE INVENTION

Historical and archeological research has provided a clear picture of how quite different cultures have tried to find solutions for their need to record language in a form that could be read and understood independently of speakers.[7] This is not the place to discuss the various attempts made to develop consistent systems of signs to represent speech. Instead, I summarize these attempts by indicating how the solutions can be ranked along a scale from signs that are entirely uncorrelated with speech sounds, to those designed to be fully correlated. Three

---

[6]A revealing history of English spelling is given by Scragg (1974).
[7]The history of writing has been described extensively by Gelb (1963) and Coulmas (1989).

types of systems have been used, where the signs represent either words, syllables, or phonemes. It is quite informative to see how different writing systems depend on the specifics of the language involved, and how they differ in terms of their advantages and disadvantages.

1. *Words as units.* As we have seen for speech development in infants, words seem to be the most obvious units for representation in written signs. This appears to hold universally for ancient as well as for recent attempts to record spoken language. Such signs start as pictographs visually related to the objects or events represented. The best known ancient examples are the Egyptian hieroglyphs in which one can recognize animals, plants, actions, and so on. The great advantage of word-based signs is that, because they are not connected to sounds, they are independent of the spoken language. Hence pictographs are still very popular as international signs. They are easy to read and can be used to represent not only single items, such as numbers or currencies, but even entire sentences, such as the traffic sign symbolizing *do not enter.*

However, for a general-purpose writing system, the disadvantages of word pictographs (or ideograms as their more abstract offsprings) considerably exceed their advantages. For example, they are useful only for small vocabularies. As mentioned earlier, it has been estimated that the average child at the age of 6 may command a lexicon of about 14,000 words, which increases to about 45,000 for high-school graduates (Miller, 1991). Such numbers indicate that although word pictographs may look promising at first, they rapidly lose their utility as vocabularies expand in this way.

Of course, there is a language, Chinese, spoken by more than one-fifth of the present world population, that uses a pictograph writing system. Its great advantage is that, notwithstanding the large differences in the sounds of dialects spoken in different parts of the country, all who learn to read Chinese can communicate in their common written language. However, great effort is required to teach beginning readers a minimum of about 8,000 signs, considered to be a necessary base for reading. Additional signs have to be looked up in a dictionary. The fact that the Chinese have maintained their ideographic system may be related to the monosyllabic nature of Chinese. Apparently, a phoneme-based writing system was never considered.

2. *Syllables as units.* Regarding the origin of the Roman alphabet, developments in the ancient Middle East and Egypt played an essential role. Scholars in these regions apparently realized quite early the limitations of pictographs. The earliest attempt to limit the number of symbols was to consider that words that sound the same, although differing in meaning, should be represented by the same sign. This can be compared with a rebus in which pictures are used having

names phonetically similar to parts of a sentence one would like to represent. Driver (1948) gave the following example in English: A row of symbols for *eye, can, knot, meat,* and *hymn* can be read as the sentence *I cannot meet him.* In English, such successful rebuses are quite rare and commonly require corrections such as adding or eliminating letters that do not fit. Thus it is understandable that similar attempts in the past were also found to be unsatisfactory.

As the languages of the Middle East and Egypt included multisyllabic words, a more promising alternative was to use syllables instead of words as units in writing. Egyptian hieroglyphs began as word pictographs, but apparently came to represent syllables rather than words. The same was true for the cuneiform signs of the Sumerians. Although this development represented a substantial reduction in the number of required signs, it was still unsuitable as a general so-lution, except for certain languages, such as Japanese, in which the words are composed of a rather limited number of different syllables, such as in *Nagasaki* and *Fujimura.* The Japanese developed a highly successful syllabic-based writing system. The very low rate of dyslexia in Japan is seen as evidence that, at least as a first stage for training children, the so-called Hiragana and Katakana systems, each consisting of 48 monosyllables (cf. Sakamoto & Makita, 1973), represent a more suitable solution for Japanese than a system based on words or phonemes.

3. *Phonemes as units.* The great breakthrough came within the family of Semitic lan-guages spoken by, among others, the Phoenicians, Hebrews, and Arabs. Most words in these languages are bisyllabic, consisting of the sequence consonant–vowel–con-sonant–vowel–consonant, without consonant clusters. The three consonants of each word can be considered as representing the roots of a family of words with closely related meanings, differing only in their vowels. For example, the vowels in s-*(vowel)*-l-*(vowel)*-m can be different, but all variants are related in meaning to the word *salem* (peace). Such relationships do not exist in English: *hat, hot,* and *hit* have quite different and unrelated meanings.

Thus the languages of the ancient Middle East were uniquely suited to de-velop a phoneme-based writing system. More than 3,000 years ago, it was dis-covered that any bisyllabic Semitic word could be represented by three signs standing for the characteristic (consonantal) speech gestures at the beginning, the center, and the end of the spoken word. Such a system can be convenient and easy to learn. For an example in English, we could use the word "two" to represent any occasion of its initial sound /t/, and the word "nine" to represent any occasion of its initial sound /n/. Thus the spoken word "tent" could be writ-ten as "292". In Phoenician, the first four consonants of the alphabet stood for the beginning of the words 'āleph (not a vowel but a weak consonant), bêth, gīmel, and dāleth, the words for *ox, house, camel,* and *door,* respectively.

The simplified example of 292 for *tent* illustrates the great advantage of an easy sound–sign conversion rule as well as the extreme reduction achieved in the number of different signs required, less than 30 for Phoenician. It had the great advantage of a very easy conversion rule combined with an extreme reduction in the number of different signs, to less than 30. The next step was made by the Greeks, who adopted the system from the Phoenicians. Although the Greek language lacked the unique structure of Semitic words, only a minor step was needed to generalize the rule by accepting abstract signs for the consonants and introducing new ones for the vowels. Thus the *alphabet* (its name recalling its Semitic origin) was born.

Thus our written alphabet is a phoneme-based system. The fact that such a system was invented only once in history, within the framework of a family of languages that were optimally suited for it, demonstrates the universal barrier against perceiving spoken words and syllables as the sums of smaller units. The unique background of our writing system confirms that even gifted observers have not been led on their own to discover phonemes as perceptual universals.

Historically, the letters of our alphabet should be seen as *instruction codes* of how words are to be pronounced. That is, they are based not on how speech is *perceived* but how it is *produced*. As it is much easier to conceptualize how the consonants are pronounced than the vowels, this may have been an additional factor in the predisposition of the Semitic languages for developing the alphabet. Along the correlation scale mentioned earlier between spoken and written language, the original alphabet represents the extreme of 100% correlation.

The statement that the letters represent instruction codes for pronouncing the written text should be taken quite literally. For most skilled readers, silent reading is the norm. The essential role of printed text in modern society demands that every adult be a highly experienced reader, able to scan texts very quickly, and this would be very difficult in a practical sense if all reading had to be done aloud. Thus we have forgotten that, originally, reading aloud was the usual practice. As Manguel (1996) wrote: St. Augustine, also a professor of rhetoric, "following the teachings of Aristotle, knew that letters, 'invented so that we might be able to converse even with the absent,' were 'signs of sounds' and these in turn were 'signs of things we think'" (p. 45). According to this author: "Until well into the Middle Ages, writers assumed that their readers would hear rather than simply see the text, much as they themselves spoke their words out loud as they composed them" (p. 47). The use of reading aloud is now limited almost exclusively to instruction for beginning readers.

For the modern skilled reader, the close relation between written letters and spoken phonemes has lost much of its significance. As the result of long training and much experience, we have a huge mental lexicon of written words so that we predominantly read words rather than letters. The slow reader of former days appears to have been quite content with texts in which the words were not separated by spaces, an accurate reflection of how words are spoken, following each other continuously. We as word readers, however, approach a written text quite differently and are greatly helped by the use of spaces to separate words:

Thiscanbeeasilyillustratedbyeliminatingthespacesasinthisssentence.

It is obviously difficult to read this sentence printed in this way, whereas we would have no difficulty if the sentence were spoken normally, that is, with no silent pauses between words. More is said about this dissimilarity between reading and listening, as well as their shared features, in the next chapter. Here, I restrict myself to noting that the history of the alphabet reveals a basic difference between letters and phonemes. Whereas letters should be seen as instructions for speech *production*, phonemes are, at least according to the "definition" given earlier in this chapter, seen as categories based on *perception*. Therefore, it is confusing to say that the written alphabet "exploits" the phoneme (Studdert-Kennedy, 1987). Written letters are *prelinguistic* signs. The phonetic alphabet, on the other hand, consists of signs designed "in such a way that no one member ever occurs in a word in the same phonetic context as any other member," (Jones, 1950/1976, p. 47) implying that they should reflect the acoustics of speech. This difference means that there is, in principle, no one-to-one correspondence between graphemes and phonemes, a fortiori, that knowing how words are written should not play a role in phoneme identification. This may seem an unimportant conclusion, but it is not. As Lüdtke (1969) concluded in his penetrating study of the origin of our alphabet, there is good reason to suppose that phoneme theory is a consequence of the invention of the alphabet.

DISCUSSION

This chapter began by describing the introduction of the spectrograph and the ways in which early speech researchers attempted to reconcile the continuous speech signal with the prevailing concept that speech consists of a succession of discrete phonemes corresponding to the letters of a written text. According to this view, the actual acoustic speech signal is a rather imperfect approximation to the speaker's intention. The vocal tract is physically unable to materialize the individual phonemes intended by the speaker so that the listener has to accept a continuous flow of sound characterized by fuzzy coarticulation rather than phonemic discreteness. Thus the listener's remarkable achievement of "rediscovering" the intended phonemes cannot be considered as a restoration, an impossible task as Hockett (1955) rightly noted. On the contrary, it was supposed to be a quite different process in which the speech sounds were interpreted in terms of the intended gestures of their production—a view culminating in the motor theory of speech perception introduced by Liberman a few years later. As we saw, attempts to prove that the acoustic signal carries sufficient information for identifying the individual phonemes have not been very convincing.

There are, however, remaining questions regarding this issue. The motor theory considers that, in view of the neural "module" required to rediscover the intended phonemes, "speech is special," and thus we should expect that speech recognition is a unique function of the human race. However, it has been demonstrated that, after appropriate training, other mammals (Kuhl, 1987a) as well as birds (Kluender, Diehl, & Killeen, 1987) can discriminate speech sounds in a way similar to human observers, a finding that does not support such uniqueness. Although this and other evidence seem to suggest that we do not need the motor theory, on the other hand, such evidence does not prove that it is wrong. The motor theory remains the most satisfactory explanation[8]—as long as one maintains that identification of the individual phonemes is a prerequisite of speech perception. Instead of spending energy in searching for direct arguments against the motor theory, it makes more sense to consider whether in fact phoneme identification is necessary for speech perception.

The experimental evidence discussed in the previous sections of this chapter suggests answers to this question. We have seen that:

1. The context of a phoneme contributes considerably to its identification, revealing that coarticulation is a positive rather than a negative factor in speech perception.

2. Young infants learn to comprehend and repeat words without being aware of phonemes.

3. The conscious awareness of phonemes appears to be associated with learning to read.

4. We owe our phoneme-based alphabet to the unique structure of a particular family of languages.

These findings strongly suggest that the concept of phonemes as units of speech perception may be more related to the experience of learning to spell words rather the reflection of a natural perceptual phenomenon. We have seen that, originally, alphabetic signs represented pronunciation instructions, and

---

[8]I do not consider Fowler's (1987) theory of direct perception a serious alternative.

they have maintained this function more or less faithfully as used in modern languages. The routine of alphabetic spelling as a cultural achievement may have biased our approach to the understanding of speech perception. It seems almost impossible to approach speech perception as a nonreader would do.

The implications of this bias are profound. It is common practice in phoneme-identification experiments to ask that the listener write down responses using alphabetic symbols. For example, let us take the syllables phonetically written as /di/ and /du/, discussed by Liberman et al. (1967). As the authors indicated, the second formant of the /d/ in the first case rises from approximately 2,200 to 2,600 Hz, whereas in the second case it falls from about 1,200 to 700 Hz. In their opinion, the two /d/s, although different acoustically, are still the same perceptually. But how can we be sure that they are perceptually the same indeed? The /d/s sounded different when presented reversed in time, so that the authors concluded: "So long as the second-formant transitions of /di/ and /du/ are not heard as speech, however, they do not sound alike" (p. 436). How can we know that the literate listeners, knowing from a long experience that the initial sounds of both syllables correspond with the same letter *d*, did not select (almost unavoidably) their written response based on this familiarity, just as they know to write the initial and final consonants of the syllable /pip/ both as *p* even though these two versions of /p/ sound quite different?

These are only two examples of what I am afraid is the *universal* disregard of the role of the listener's spelling knowledge in word identification tests in which the listeners have to write down the word they believe to have heard. Can we really expect that the listeners will set this knowledge aside in giving their response? If I were to ask a foreigner[9] to spell the Dutch word *angstschreeuw* (/ɑŋstsɣreːʊ/, cry of distress) as pronounced by a native speaker, probably no one would succeed, whereas it is an easy task for a Dutch listener who knows how the word is written.

As illiterate listeners are hard to find, the actual role of spelling ability in such experiments can be difficult to assess. It seems to me that the experiments with preschool children and adult nonreaders mentioned earlier in this chapter offer a preliminary answer to this question. The fact that the listeners were not able to recognize the same consonant presented in different contexts confirms the confounding role of spelling ability in speech identification tests. Therefore, identically spelled responses in identification tests cannot be trusted as indicating that perceptually identical sounds were heard.

---

[9]Germans excluded who have the word *Angstschrei* with the same meaning.

Additional evidence can be found in experiments in which young children are asked to segment consonant clusters. Ehri and Wilce (1980) found that, whereas most children who had learned to read were able to do this task, preschool children could not. The younger children perceived consonant clusters as single sounds. The authors concluded that the "reader's conceptualization of the phonemic structure of words is influenced by knowledge of word spellings" (p. 379).

It is interesting to speculate how our ideas of basic speech units might have developed if the sound spectrograph had been invented not in our alphabetized world but in China. In that case, the continuous spectrograms of speech utterances might have led to a quite different theory of speech perception with basic units larger than phonemes. Because the written characters of Chinese can be seen as corresponding with monosyllabic words (a first-order approximation), it is likely that Chinese speech scientists would have accepted the word as the basic unit of speech.

It is remarkable that the impact of our alphabetic writing system on the theory of speech perception has been underestimated or even overlooked by so many speech scientists. The traditional position of the phoneme seems to be much more axiomatic than that it can be accepted as based on experimental evidence. Happily, some rare passages in the literature can be found in which the prevailing view of the phoneme's dominant role in speech perception has been questioned. Ladefoged (1967), after having cited adherents of discrete phonemes, concluded:

> Nevertheless, there is, in fact, very little experimental evidence for the assumption that there are discrete units involved in the production and perception of speech which corresponds to phonemes. There are certainly no natural, self-evident, segments of speech of this size; and no one has yet succeeded in describing a set of either articulatory or acoustic segments.... There is no reason to suppose that people perceive incoming sensory data in terms of the same units as they later use for describing it, since they then use other knowledge provided by their competence in the language.... The belief that the units involved in the production and perception of speech are discrete elements of the size of a phoneme is reinforced by the fact that we are accustomed to describing speech in terms of alphabetic writing. This system of analyzing speech and reducing it to a convenient visual form has had a considerable influence on western thought about the nature of speech. (pp. 145–147)

Some years later, Repp (1981) wrote:

> These units [phonetic segments, RP] are *abstractions*. They are the end result of complex perceptual and cognitive processes in the listener's brain, and it is likely that, excluding certain laboratory tasks, they are in fact not perceptual primitives but are derived by cognitive analysis from larger units, such as syllables or words.... Moreover,

it appears that their conscious perception presupposes familiarity with an alphabetic writing system. (p. 1462)

This agrees with the concise statement by Nooteboom (1981) that "word recognition is not mediated by phonemes but, on the contrary, phoneme identification is mediated by word recognition" (p. 147). Probably Warren (1981) is the one who expressed himself most explicitly contra the phoneme as the unit in speech perception:

> I would like to spell out some reasons why I believe the phoneme is basically an articulatory unit, not a perceptual unit. The phoneme appears to be linked conceptually to the alphabet as a set of instructions for speech production. An unfamiliar word can be articulated simply by proceeding through the series of instructions given by the letters within a word (at least for languages in which spelling has not diverged as far from pronunciation as in English). The brilliant unknown inventor of the alphabet must have carefully observed the limited number of articulatory gestures associated with a particular language, and produced a separate symbol for each. (p. 35)

Finally, I may quote recent reflections by Nygaard and Pisoni (1995):

> Since most research in speech perception has concentrated on the segmental analysis of phonemes, there has always been a wide gap between research conducted on the perception of isolated segments and the role of prosodic factors in the processing of connected speech. (p. 74)

After having referred to the variations in speaker and in speech rate, they concluded:

> Taken together, the research on these factors suggests that traditional explanations of speech perception may need to reconsider their long-standing emphasis on the search for abstract, canonical linguistic units as the end point of perception.... Indeed, the study of speech has concentrated almost exclusively on laboratory experiments designed to evaluate the perception of speech produced by a single speaker in an acoustically sterile environment. The consequence of this approach has been the neglect of issues relating to perceptual organization. (pp. 75–76)

In most of these quotations, the position of the phoneme in speech is seen as derived from the role of letters in writing. Ladefoged referred to Gelb's (1963) book on the origin of writing, and Repp to Lüdtke's (1969) study on the relation between phonetic segments and the alphabet.

The experimental evidence presented in this chapter strongly suggests that consonants and vowels *in combination*—that is, syllables or words—are better candidates for basic units in the perception of speech than single phonemes are. Considering the word as the basic speech unit makes it possible to describe speech production and perception within a much more general sensorimotor context.

For instance, to articulate a word such as /bæg/, we shape the vocal tract as required for the vowel, start the syllable by opening the lips, and then complete it by touching the back of the tongue to the soft palate. If we described the result as though it were produced with a musical instrument, for example, a trumpet, we would say that the "tone" of the syllable is a sound pulse characterized by a certain onset and an offset. Why should speech sounds be interpreted differently from the sounds made with musical instruments? Why not say that the /b/ and /g/ are specific ways to start and stop a particular complex tone? Reasoning along these lines transforms coarticulation from a disturbing interaction into a natural spectrotemporal variation pattern determined by the way in which a syllabic speech sound needs to begin and end. Stetson (1951) advocated this view half a century ago; however, almost nobody seems to have heard his voice.

Such an approach highlights a fundamental difference between vowels and consonants. Perhaps nowhere is this difference more clear than in vocal music, where all notes are carried on the vowels, the syllabic nuclei. The periodic vibrations of the vocal cords can be compared with the carrier of radio waves. The vocal tract *modulates* these waves spectrotemporally. The fact that whispered speech is perfectly intelligible demonstrates that a periodic carrier is not essential—the main contribution of the voice is to increase the loudness and, consequently, the intelligibility of the speech signal. As reflected in the origins of the alphabet reviewed earlier, speech information is primarily embodied in the consonants—the temporal pattern of modulation of the speech carrier. The more sustained parts of the carrier can also be shaped to create the distinctions of different vowels. The great freedom of vowel spectra in actual speech, manifest in large overlaps as is shown in the next chapter, illustrates the secondary role of vowels in speech perception. Wrttn spch wtht vwls cn b rd, i oe o o o ee iou ooa (written speech without vowels can be read, which does not hold for speech without consonants).

There is also the consideration that the list of accepted phonemes seems to be rather arbitrary. The phonetic alphabet reflects the tacit presupposition that speech sounds are much more characterized by some steady-state spectrum than by their temporal structure. Whereas it can be defended that many phonemes have a steady-state kernel, some definitely have not; the /ŋ/ of *ping*, the /ʃ/ of *shoe*, the /tʃ/ of *catch*, and the /dʒ/ of *judge* have a dynamic structure incompatible with the discreteness concept; their definition as single phonemes rather than as phoneme pairs has a linguistic rather than a perceptual basis. Other sounds, such as the stop consonants, are even more completely characterized by their temporal properties.

The reader will have noticed that in this chapter relatively little attention has been paid to the cognitive aspects of speech perception, and to the fact that we are usually listening to words and sentences in a language with which we are familiar, which means that both *prediction* and *recognition* play an important role. Whereas this chapter has presented predominantly indirect evidence that syllables and words rather than phonemes are the basic units of speech perception, the next chapter provides ample direct evidence of the contributory role of cognitive factors.

CONCLUSIONS

The introduction of the spectrograph half a century ago can be seen as the beginning of modern speech research, much of which has addressed the question of how listeners are able to derive the discrete phonemes intended by the speaker from the continuous speech signal. Later research raised doubts about the phoneme as the basic unit in the perception of speech, citing observations that coarticulation actually contributes in a positive way to the identification of phonemes and that learning to read an alphabetic writing system appears to aid listeners in becoming aware of the existence of phonemes.

From this evidence, supplemented with our knowledge of how the alphabet came into existence, we may conclude that the concept of phonemes as basic units in speech perception has been strongly biased by our familiarity with the written alphabet. It seems more likely that syllables and words rather than phonemes are the real perceptual units of speech. We need to turn next to a consideration of the intelligibility of fluent speech to find the answer to this question.

5
Speech Perception 2: The Intelligibility of Fluent Speech

As an introduction to this study, I discussed in chapter 1 some preferences of scientists in designing experiments. The first was to concentrate on manageable small subsystems with a minimal number of parameters. Another, related to the former, was to exclude in "clean" experiments the disturbing factors of the outside world as much as possible. Both preferences were amply present in the investigations discussed in the previous chapter. There, attention was primarily concentrated on small speech segments: phonemes, syllables, and words, not disturbed by other sounds.

These restrictions have had clear advantages and have helped us acquire a better insight into the role of phonemes in speech perception. Although these experiments suggested that syllables and words rather than individual phonemes are better candidates for perceptual units, no entirely convincing conclusion could be drawn. It may be that as long as we stay at the "elemental" level, it will remain difficult to reach a definite conclusion. We may have to focus our attention on larger speech segments, such as sentences, to get a true picture of how speech is actually perceived. Moreover, as shown later, such a focus may be revealing regarding the ways in which speech resists interference from other sounds.

There is another important reason to study larger segments: speech perception includes the *recognition* of what has been said, an essential aspect that cannot play its full role as long as only "manageable small subsystems" are considered. If the recognition of spoken words were the result of the correct identification of a string of successive phonemes, the study of subsystems would be sufficient to explain speech intelligibility. However, the reality is much more complex.

Sentences rather than single words are the everyday units of speech communication. Using a limited, albeit very large, number of words, each based on a rather restricted set of articulatory gestures, we are able to compose an endless number of different sentences. Even when we utter a single word such as "yes," it can stand for much more than just a positive sign; it is the shortest possible summary of expressing agreement with what has been said. Investigators evaluating the quality of speech communication systems are primarily interested in how faithfully these systems preserve the spectrotemporal variations of the signal required for correct speech understanding. As a result, it is the intelligibility of sentences that is their main interest. The points of departure of the more theoretically oriented scientist studying the perception of single speech segments, and the more practically oriented engineer investigating the intelligibility of much larger units, are so different that, as the literature shows, the mutual interest in each other's approaches and achievements has been considerably less than should have been true for two branches of the same discipline.

The fact that single words represent the smallest meaningful units of speech as well as the shortest "sentences" indicates that the word is the meeting point of two subdisciplines. In this chapter most attention is directed to the question of how well sentences are perceived. This does not mean that we lose sight of words, syllables, and phonemes. Particularly in the beginning, we need them for a better view regarding their role in sentence intelligibility. However, we may find that in the confrontation between the more elementalistic approach of basic research and the more holistic one of applied research, the elementalistic approach has to be called into question.

THE VARIANCE OF THE SPEECH SIGNAL

Speech intelligibility means recognition. We may hear a garbled sentence or only a single word and, on the basis of previous experience, are able to recognize what has been said. The problem is that no two utterances of the same speech fragment are acoustically equal. This holds for words pronounced by the same speaker but even more so for words pronounced by different speakers. We should realize that, although speech production is primarily an *analog* process resulting in a signal that can vary spectrally continuously in time, recognition as a form of classification is a *digital* process resulting in categorical decisions. In other words: A *variant* stimulus has to be converted into an *invariant* response. Hence, the question can be asked: How much variance is allowed in the stimulus before the flexibility of the response is exhausted?

This question has been primarily studied for vowel sounds. It has been known for a long time that, as a consequence of dimensional differences in the vocal tracts of men, women, and children, the formant frequencies of vowels produced by each group differ systematically. As an illustration, Fig. 5.1 represents the frequencies of the first two formants, averaged over five subjects of each group, of nine vowels segmented from syllables such as /pip/, /pIp/, and others (Strange, Verbrugge, Shankweiler, & Edman, 1976). We see that the overlap is so considerable that the same configuration of formants may correspond with different vowels for the three categories of speakers.

In their paper, the authors also presented identification scores for different groups of listeners. They observed that 69% of the vowels were correctly identified if all vowels presented were taken from the same speaker category, but only 57% if vowel sounds of men, women, and children were mixed. Apparently, the perceptual adaptation to the characteristic differences, particularly the fundamental frequency of the vocal chords, was more effective in the first than in the latter case. Although proposals have been put forward to explain the perceptual invariance of vowels pronounced by different speakers in terms of formant-frequency ratios rather than their absolute values (e.g., Ladefoged & Broadbent, 1957; Miller, 1989), we should not overlook that about one out of three of the unmixed vowels was not correctly identified. If such a considerable uncertainty

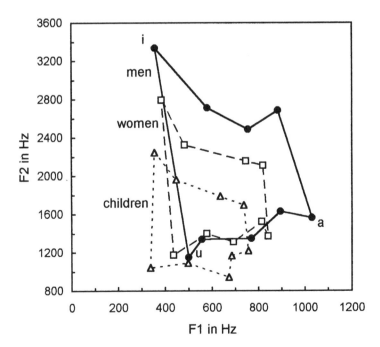

FIG. 5.1.   Average formant frequencies F2 versus F1 for 9 isolated vowels spoken by men, women, and children (based on data from Strange et al., 1976).

is experienced for vowels in isolated words, we can be sure that it will be even larger for vowels in connected discourse.

The difference between the scores for segregated versus mixed vowel lists illustrates the capacity of the speech-recognition process for coping with systematic differences between voices. It appears that hearing even a few words can be sufficient for a listener to "tune in" to the characteristics of a particular voice. Early evidence for this process was presented in a classic investigation by Ladefoged and Broadbent (1957). They synthesized six versions of the sentence "Please say what this word is", differing according to the ranges of variation of the first and second formants. Additionally, four test words of the form b(vowel)t were synthesized, again based on different formant frequencies. Listeners heard the sentences followed by the words and had to decide whether the word bit, bet, bat, or but had been presented. The results showed that the identification of the word-medial vowel depended on the version of the preceding sentence. The listeners apparently used the introductory sentence to "tune in" to the specific formant structure of each (artificial) speaker, as a guide for listening to the vowel of the following word. The experiment nicely illustrates how listeners unconsciously adapt a reference framework for phonemes, based on word recognition of previous items. It also demonstrates the power of the recognition process for coping with spectral variance.[1]

We are so familiar with the fact that, irrespective of large interspeaker differences in accent, pitch, and loudness, we almost "automatically" know what a speaker says, that the question of uncertainty may seem relevant only in cases when the speech signal is severely mutilated by distortion or disturbed by other sounds. This may be the reason that most speech research has focused on the perception and identification of phonemes in well-pronounced words, whereas almost no attention has been given to the identification of phonemes as they are pronounced under everyday conditions in sentences.

It is easy to spell out spoken sentences, even if they are extracted from conversational speech. As a result, we may be inclined to think that in everyday situations, the identity of phonemes is quite well preserved. However, this is in fact a rather naive conclusion because it overlooks the important role played by our knowledge about how words are written. As discussed in the previous chapter, we are so familiar with phoneme–grapheme conversion and the way in which words are spelled that it seems as if all spoken phonemes are readily identifiable. This factor can be eliminated by listening to sentences in an unfamiliar language, where semantic and linguistic knowledge are of no help. Such an experi-

---

[1]Nygaard and Pisoni (1995) presented data on the variability of speech sounds in their excellent review.

ment was performed by Shockey and Reddy (1975), who found that four phoneticians could correctly transcribe in phonetic symbols only 56% of the phonemes of a spoken foreign language, and additionally, that there was 50% disagreement in transcriptions from different phoneticians.

There are numerous studies on the identification of isolated vowels or vowels pronounced in carefully controlled syllables, but data on the identification of vowels extracted from fluent speech appear to be almost absent. The study by Koopmans-van Beinum (1980), based on Dutch texts, is a rare exception. I restrict myself to a comparison of her data for isolated vowels and vowels extracted from recordings of free conversation. Figure 5.2 presents the F1–F2 plots, averaged over two male and two female speakers. The smaller vowel area is based on the mean values for stressed and unstressed extracted vowels. The ellipses represent the mean standard deviations of repeated pronunciations by

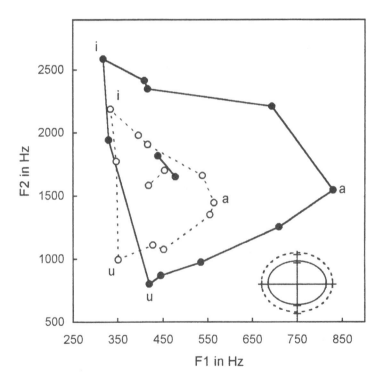

FIG. 5.2.   Average formant frequencies F1 versus F2 for 12 isolated vowels (solid symbols) and vowels extracted from free conversation (open symbols). The ellipses give the mean standard deviation of repeated pronunciations by the same speaker (based on data from Koopmans-van Beinum, 1980).

the same speaker. Compared with isolated pronunciations, the spectral area covered by the vowels shrinks by about a factor 3 whereas the area of the ellipses increases by about a factor of 2. Based on these differences, we might guess that the number of identification errors will differ by a factor of 6. In fact, an identification test of the vowel sounds, with separate lists for each speaker, showed an increase from 10.4% mean error score for isolated vowels to 67.0% for vowels extracted from free conversation (10 different extracts of each vowel; 100 listeners), corresponding with a factor 6.3, a surprisingly good agreement with the rough prediction based on differences in spectral spread and variation.

These results, of both the formant analysis and the listening tests, demonstrate that, despite speaker normalization, the spectral variance of vowels is so large that the excellent recognizability of fluent speech, suggesting invariant vowel identification, cannot be explained by the acoustic specification of the speech signal as such. As discussed later, other factors play an important role. The variations in pronunciation in everyday situations are predictably so large that we must be cautious in drawing general conclusions based on rather abstract laboratory experiments with carefully pronounced stimuli.

The speech signal is not only highly variant in terms of its spectrum, but also in terms of its temporal structure. This holds for differences between speakers as well as for intra-speaker variation. Spectral variance is most important for vowels, whereas temporal variance is crucial in consonant identification. It is remarkable that, as contrasted with spectral variance, temporal variance is traditionally considered as representing no problem for speech intelligibility, unusually fast speaking excluded. However, systems of automatic speech recognition appear to have great difficulties with temporal uncertainties of the speech elements, again suggesting that the appearance of effortlessness may underestimate the accomplishments of perception.

An analysis of connected discourse from 30 speakers, carried out by Miller, Grosjean, and Lomanto (1984), gave some information regarding acoustic differences related to rate of articulation. This rate was defined in terms of average syllable duration. From their summary of the data we can conclude that the average syllable duration across all speakers was 216 msec, with a standard deviation of 25 msec. The syllable durations for different productions from the same speaker exhibited standard deviations that ranged between 31 and 121 msec, with a mean value of 67 msec. Thus the within-speaker standard deviation in articulation rate was two to three times larger than the between-speaker standard deviation. Whereas the average syllable duration was, as mentioned, 216 msec, the difference in syllable duration of the fastest and the slowest runs of the individual speakers appeared to be even more than 300 msec.

Extensive data on the duration of individual phonemes in connected discourse were collected by Crystal and House. In Fig. 5.3 results on the duration of vowels and consonants are summarized (Crystal & House, 1990). As we see, the average duration of a vowel is essentially independent of the number of initial and final consonants, whereas the total duration of the syllable increases almost linearly with the number of consonants. A typical average duration of vowels is 120 msec and of consonants 80 msec. An earlier paper (Crystal & House, 1988a) provided data on the duration of (long) vowels in connected discourse of six speakers, indicating that the differences in duration of the same vowel pronounced by the same speaker in different contexts can be more than three times larger than the spread of the average vowel duration between speakers (38% vs. 11%).

In a subsequent study, Crystal and House (1988b) investigated the duration of stop consonants in connected discourse. Measurements indicated that only 45% could be considered as "complete stops," that is, including an identifiable occlusion followed by a plosive burst. The authors concluded that differences between stop consonants observed "in formal experiments with balanced word materials" are not strongly evident in connected speech.

Another way of studying perceptual flexibility with respect to speech is by investigating the extent to which the spectrum and speed of recorded speech can be manipulated before speech becomes unintelligible. Experiments have shown that shifts of a factor of two in spectral features (Morrow, 1971) as well as in time can be tolerated.

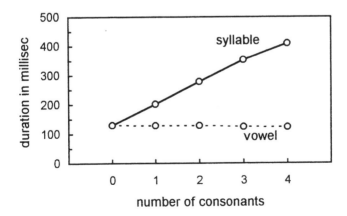

FIG. 5.3.   Average duration of (stressed) vowels and syllables in connected discourse as a function of the number of consonants (based on data from Crystal & House, 1990).

These results demonstrate that spectral as well as temporal characteristics distinguishing vowels and consonants presented as isolated phonemes are not as available in fluent speech. The variation of characteristic parameters appears to be so large that their information content is insufficient for identifying single phonemes, just as the data from Shockey and Reddy (1975) and Koopmans-van Beinum (1980) confirmed. If speech fragments themselves are not sufficient for phoneme identification, it is reasonable that the semantic and linguistic content of larger units provides the required information.

THE REDUNDANCY OF THE SPEECH SIGNAL

The finding that only a minority of phonemes in conversational speech are unambiguously identifiable on the basis of acoustical content alone clearly indicates that if speech intelligibility were determined exclusively by phoneme identification, conversation would be impossible. This is not just a guess: The first unsuccessful attempts to develop automatic speech-recognition systems unequivocally demonstrated that this conclusion is correct. Nevertheless, our daily experience tells us that conversational speech is perceived easily. Even when we speak in a rather sloppy manner, we are usually well understood. Apparently, speech perception involves much more intelligent processes than a simple sequential identification of successive sound segments.

The reader will recall from the previous chapter that syllables and words are much better candidates for the smallest units in speech perception than are phonemes. Hence, it is tempting to solve our problem by suggesting that speech intelligibility is the result of recognizing words rather than identifying phonemes—once the listener has learned the meaning of a huge number of spoken words, this would be sufficient to make fluent speech intelligible. However, even speech segments of word duration, when isolated from their conversational context, can be too short for unambiguous recognition. So the substitution of words for phonemes as the building blocks of speech cannot fully explain speech intelligibility. Our ability to understand speech is the most striking demonstration that the perception of sound depends on cognitive as well as auditory processes.

We can distinguish different degrees by which cognitive factors are involved in sound perception. The role of cognition can be minimal in listening to simple sounds such as single tone bursts. Next, the identification of phonemes requires some cognitive component in the form of an internal reference system, albeit a rather small one. For word recognition, appeals to the mental lexicon represent a much larger reference system involving much more complex sounds. Finally, the interpretation of sentences and paragraphs may be considered to represent the highest level of sound perception, in which all possible cognitive information sources (semantic, prosodic, lexical, syntactic) are mobilized.

Before presenting data documenting the insufficiency of single words and the need for context for obtaining intelligible speech, discussed in the next section, it may be worthwhile to give some quantitative impression of how large the redundancy of the speech signal appears to be.

Redundancy means that speech can be reduced substantially in information content before losing its identity. In other words, normal speech has a surplus of intelligibility. The score of 100% is a ceiling effect, concealing the fact that, in a manner of speaking, the theoretical "true" score may be considerably higher. The phenomenon of redundancy indicates the role of cognition in speech understanding. We can obtain some impression of the amount of redundancy by investigating the extent to which the speech signal can be degraded before becoming unintelligible.

There are many ways in which speech can be degraded. The most common examples in everyday practice are reductions in frequency range, smoothing of temporal fluctuations by reverberation, and masking of the weaker parts of the speech signal by noise. As the information in the signal is primarily determined by variations in frequency and time, it seems to be most appropriate to study speech redundancy by investigating the degree to which such spectral and temporal fluctuations can be reduced before actually affecting intelligibility. These fluctuations are the primary clues by which sounds are discriminated and their detection represents basic properties of the auditory system.

Spectral Smearing

We saw in chapter 2 that the ear's frequency resolution is determined by critical bandwidths equal to f/f values of about 20% (between ¼ and ⅓ octave). The phenomenon of redundancy suggests that this resolution is larger than required to understand undisturbed speech. As it is impossible to change the ear's critical bands, we can try to simulate this by reducing the spectral structure of the incoming sounds. For example, by degrading the speech signal in such a way that spectral differences within an octave are fully smoothed, we can simulate (at least with respect to intelligibility) an ear with critical bands that are one octave wide. A signal-processing algorithm to perform such spectral smearing was developed by ter Keurs (ter Keurs, Festen, & Plomp, 1992).

Of primary interest is the maximal bandwidth over which the speech signal can be smeared before becoming unintelligible. Ter Keurs (ter Keurs, Festen, &

Plomp, 1993) found that meaningful sentences even when smeared over four octaves were 100% correctly understood. This result reveals that critical bands that are more than 12 times wider than in normal hearing would still allow us to understand sentences in quiet. In a comparable experiment, Baer and Moore (1993) observed no effect on the intelligibility of sentences presented in quiet for their maximal smearing condition using bandwidths six times wider that the critical band.

A quite different approach was followed by investigators who wanted to determine how many electrodes are required in cochlear implants to transfer the essential information of the speech signal to a deaf person. Shannon, Zeng, Kamath, Wygonski, and Ekelid (1995) and Dorman, Loizou, and Rainey (1997) divided the speech range into a number of frequency channels and replaced each of them by a noise band provided with the same temporal envelope as the original speech band. Sentences processed in this way were presented to normal-hearing listeners. Figure 5.4 shows that only four to five frequency channels were required for listeners to recognize almost all words correctly. As may be expected, the corresponding bandwidth of about one octave is substantially narrower than the four octaves allowed for smeared sentences. This discrepancy can be explained by the fact that in the latter case much more speech information was preserved, such as the voice pitch, and by the distinction between voiced and unvoiced phonemes.

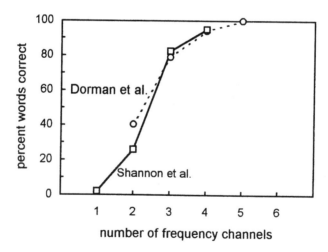

FIG. 5.4.   Recognition score of words in sentences as a function of the number of noise bands provided with the temporal envelope of the corresponding speech-frequency band (based on data from Shannon et al. ,1995, and Dorman et al., 1997).

Temporal Smearing

In a comparable way, the effect of reducing the temporal fluctuations of the speech signal was studied by Drullman (Drullman, Festen, & Plomp, 1994). Whereas ter Keurs had to apply the spectral smearing to short-time speech segments in order to avoid direct effects on the temporal structure of the signal, in Drullman's experiments the temporal smearing had to be applied to frequency bands narrower than the ear's critical bands to avoid direct effects on the spectral structure. Therefore, Drullman split up the speech signal in ¼ octaves and smeared the amplitude envelope of each frequency band separately. He found that, even with all temporal envelope fluctuations above 4 Hz eliminated, meaningful sentences in quiet were 100% correctly understood.

The smearing studies of ter Keurs and Drullman also included experiments with isolated syllables. These tests showed that consonants are much more resistant to spectral smearing than are vowels (scores of 69% for the consonants vs. 26% for the vowels, smeared over two octaves), whereas the opposite holds for temporal smearing (scores of 55% of the consonants vs. 80% of the vowels for a cutoff frequency of 2 Hz). As would be expected, the stop consonants in particular are sensitive to temporal smearing. These data confirm not only that consonants are the primary carriers of speech information, but also that their temporal characteristics (including voicing) are much more important than their spectral characteristics. These observations help explain why the speech signal can withstand very strong spectral distortions. Fluent speech with all components removed either above or below 1,500 Hz, or with spectral tilts of −12 or +12 dB per octave (van Dijkhuizen, Anema, & Plomp, 1987), is still intelligible. In both cases the temporal characteristics are quite well preserved.

It is interesting to compare the finding that consonants as the main carriers of speech intelligibility are quite susceptible to temporal smearing with the early ideas concerning the utility of the spectrograph, discussed in the previous chapter. It is clear that the spectrogram, as its name implies, represents spectral information much better than temporal information. Thus, given the evidence that temporal aspects of the signal are much more important for speech intelligibility than spectral aspects (cf. Lauter & Hirsh, 1985), it is not surprising that the original expectations for the spectrograph did not materialize.

In 1981, Remez, Rubin, Pisoni, and Carrell reported on a phenomenon that they and other scientists found puzzling. They observed that three simultaneous sinusoids that tracked the center frequencies of the lower three formants were sufficient for a group of listeners to recognize on average more than 70% of the words of the sentence "Where were you a year ago?" In subsequent reports (e.g., Remez & Rubin, 1984), the authors continued to express their surprise at the

phenomenon, which seemingly confirmed the major role of the formant frequencies as the carriers of speech information. However, it is notable that more
recent data (see Fig. 5.4) do not support that conclusion. Three sinusoids with
fixed frequencies (or fixed noise bands), which are modulated by the temporal
envelope of the speech signal within three frequency bands, appear to yield
equally high intelligibility scores. A direct comparison of the two conditions
confirms that their information content is indeed comparable with respect to
intelligibility (Breeuwer & Plomp, 1986), clearly contradicting the supposed
unique role of formant frequencies for speech perception.

The data on temporal smearing also lead to interesting observations regarding the critical property by which stop consonants are distinguished. The stops
are by far the most vulnerable consonants in cases of temporal smearing; nevertheless, it is surprising that with a lowpass cutoff frequency of 8 Hz nearly all stop
consonants could be correctly identified, and even for cutoff frequencies as low
as 2 and 4 Hz, /t/–/d/ and /p/–/b/ mistakes were almost absent. As most
voice-onset time differences between same-place voiced and unvoiced stops in-
volve less than 20 msec, we can assume that these subtle temporal differences
did not survive the temporal smearing process. This means that correct stop
identifications must have been based on perceptual differences other than
voice onset time. Experiments with whispered syllables support this view. In this
case voicing is absent but, nevertheless, 68% of voiced stops can still be correctly identified as voiced (Tartter, 1989). The voice onset time factor in stop
consonants has received much attention from phoneticians, but we might wonder whether all this effort was worthwhile.

THE SIGNIFICANCE OF CONTEXT

We saw in the previous section that fluent speech is highly redundant and that
considerable spectral and temporal smearing can be tolerated before sentences
become unintelligible. These facts demonstrate the prominent role of cognitive
factors in speech perception. Thanks to years of training and experience, we are
able to recognize sequences of speech sounds pronounced in quite different
ways and/or affected by various severe distortions, still as meaningful speech.
Audition as well as cognition is essential to achieve this result. Audition concerns the ways in which the sound stimulus is processed both peripherally and
more centrally so that its specific characteristics are preserved. Cognition concerns the way in which our previous experience with speech is used to interpret
the new signals. These two components of the process are frequently denoted as
the *bottom-up* and *top-down* aspects of perception, respectively.

Speech redundancy also refers to the fact that the "final" interpretation of a speech segment depends not only on the information included in the segment itself, but also on contextual information provided by preceding and even following speech segments. For example, it may be difficult to recognize the word *large* taken out of a sentence, whereas the word is hard not to hear if the entire sentence *He lived in a large house* is presented.

The first experimental research on the significance of context for word perception was reported a century ago. In 1900–1901, William Chandler Bagley (1874–1946)[2] published a pioneering study carried out with the newly invented Edison phonograph. His results are so interesting that it is worthwhile to give them ample attention here. Bagley's approach was inspired by Cattell's work with written speech material, discussed later in this chapter. He recorded a large number of "mutilated" words, such as monosyllables pronounced without the initial or final consonant, and longer words lacking some medial consonant. Eight members of the psychology department of Cornell University listened to these words presented either in isolation or incorporated in sentences. Bagley's conclusions are so complete that I cite the first eight in his own words:

1. In monosyllabic words the elision of the initial consonant affects perception more than the elision of the final consonant.
2. When mutilated words are given with a minimum of context, the chances for their correct perception are increased by 82% as compared with their chances of correct perception when given without context.
3. The fact of mutilation is readily noticed in the single words given without context, even though the word be finally correctly perceived; the elision is not so readily noted when the word is given with a minimum of context.
4. Polysyllabic words when mutilated are more easily recognized than monosyllabic words under the same conditions, but, when given in context, are not helped by the context as much as are the monosyllabic words.
5. When mutilated words are placed at or near the beginning of complete sentences, the chances for their correct perception are increased remarkably, the amount of increase varying with the character of the word, being greater for monosyllables and less for polysyllables.
6. When mutilated words are placed in the middle of complete sentences, there is a slight but significant increase in the percentage of correct perceptions as compared with the perceptions of the similar words placed at the beginning of complete sentences.
7. When mutilated words are placed in the middle of complete sentences, they are much more amenable to correct interpretation than when given without context.
8. The position most favorable for the correct perception of a mutilated word is at the close of a complete sentence. (pp. 94–98)

---

[2]Some biographical data were provided by Cole and Rudnicky (1983).

I fully agree with the comment made by Cole and Rudnicky (1983) when they rediscovered Bagley's report:

> Although Bagley's article was a pleasure to read, it also forced us to consider a serious and disturbing question: What really has been accomplished in the past 80 years? What do we know about speech perception in 1982 that was not reported in 1900–1901?
>
> After considering this question for the past year, we offer the following opinion: Most of the important facts about spoken-word recognition were catalogued by Bagley in 1900–1901; subsequent research has added little to this basic catalogue. In terms of identifying new phenomena, or extending our understanding of the fundamental mechanisms underlying spoken-language comprehension, precious little has come to light since Bagley's time. (p. 99)

Nevertheless, we might examine what post-Bagley investigators had to say. Miller, Heise, and Lichten (1951) seem to have been the first to reconsider the questions posed by Bagley a half century earlier. They presented their listeners with sentences containing five key words and counted the number of key words perceived correctly. Then the key words were extracted from the sentences and presented in isolation. In all tests, sentences and words were heard against a background of noise presented at different speech-to-noise ratios. The results are plotted in Fig. 5.5. These data suggest that, at all ratios, the semantic information represented by the context of the sentences contributed substantially to

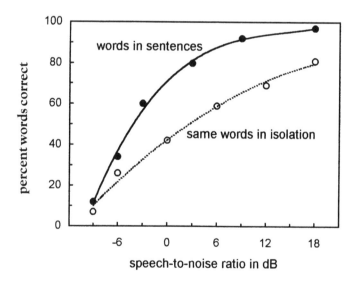

FIG. 5.5.   Identification scores of the same words spoken in isolation and in sentences as a function of speech-to-noise ratio (redrawn from Miller, Heise, & Lichten, 1951).

the recognition of the key words. Much research has been devoted to studying this process in more detail. Some results are discussed here.

One early experiment throwing additional light on the role of context in speech perception dealt with the effect of segment duration on the intelligibility of words in fluent speech (Pickett & Pollack, 1963). The authors extracted passages of three to seven words out of texts read at normal speed by four speakers and presented these passages to 15 listeners in such a way that they heard successively more words of each passage. The solid points in Fig. 5.6 summarize the results in terms of the average percentage of correctly understood words in fragments containing one, two, or three words.

The same authors investigated conversational speech in a similar way (Pollack & Pickett, 1963). The open points in Fig. 5.6 represent the average word scores for sentence fragments containing up to eight words. We see that text fragments of at least 1 sec were required to recognize correctly nearly all words. Experiments with different speech rates indicated that the total duration of a fragment rather than the number of words appeared to be the critical measure; as a result, the data here have been plotted as a function of average fragment duration. Thus a "window" of at least 1 sec is required to recognize almost all words correctly.

One major outcome of this work, surprisingly not discussed by the authors, is that word intelligibility appeared to be (almost) independent of the position of

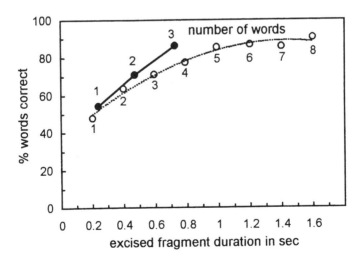

FIG. 5.6.   Average identification score of words in fragments excised from read texts (solid symbols) and conversational speech (open symbols) as a function of fragment duration (based on data from Pickett & Pollack, 1963, and Pollack & Pickett, 1963).

the target within the gated speech fragment. This implies that the recognition of a word is aided not only by *preceding* words but, to an almost equal extent, by *following* words. Later research with more sophisticated experimental paradigms has confirmed that word recognition benefits from not only preceding but also later syntactic and semantic information.

An experiment reported by Grosjean (1985) serves to illustrate this. He used sentences beginning with *I saw the*, followed by the target word, a preposition, an article, and an appropriate noun, such as "I saw the *doe* in the woods." In repeated presentations more and more of the sentence was presented. The upper boundaries of the dashed areas in Fig. 5.7 represent the percentage of the listeners who guessed correctly, and the lower boundaries denote the percentage who were absolutely confident about the target word, after having heard the sentence up to and including the target word, the following preposition, the article, and the final noun, respectively. We see that in almost all cases listeners needed more than the one-syllable target word to be sure of its identity. Even the preposition and the article were not sufficient for 25% of them. All listeners were fully confident only when the entire sentence (through the final noun) had been heard. As could be expected, the situation was much more favorable (i.e., less context was needed) for words consisting of two or three syllables.

A different approach was reported by Warren and Warren (1970). Listeners were presented with sentences such as:

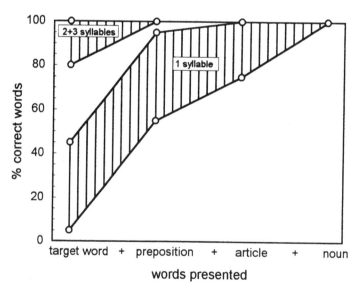

FIG. 5.7.   Average identification score of the target word in sentences as a function of the number of words presented (based on data from Grosjean, 1985).

It was found that the ■eel was on the axle.
It was found that the ■eel was on the shoe.
It was found that the ■eel was on the orange.
It was found that the ■eel was on the table.

where the symbol ■ represents a loud cough used to replaced the speech sound. Listeners reported that they heard the ■eel word with the semantically most appropriate phoneme restored: *wheel, heel, peel,* or *meal,* respectively, suggesting that even words occurring well after a mutilated fragment can contribute to a meaningful restoration.

These results, as well as data from other experiments with conversational speech (Bard, Shillcock, & Altmann, 1988), demonstrate that both preceding and later words in a sentence context are important for the recognition of a word. The analysis reported by Kučera and Francis (1967) indicated that about 64% of written text consists of monosyllabic words. As a result, we may expect that the lower dashed area in Fig. 5.7 refers to at least two-third of words spoken in conversation, suggesting that this area rather than the one for longer words actually dominates in everyday speech situations. Moreover, we need to take into account that everyday conditions are much less ideal than in these laboratory experiments with their clearly pronounced sentences, the exclusive use of nouns as stimulus words, and long response times, such as the 8 sec allowed by Grosjean (1985). On the other hand, the words prior to the target word were in Grosjean's experiment too neutral to contribute to the decision. Nevertheless, it appears justified to draw the conclusion that a considerable fraction of the words in sentences are only recognized after the next few words have been heard. The significance of later words is supported by the fact that only 40% of words are uniquely defined before their offset (Luce, 1986).

Taken together, these results demonstrate that word recognition in connected discourse cannot be purely sequential as has been assumed in the *cohort* model proposed by Marslen-Wilson (e.g., Marslen-Wilson & Welsh, 1978; criticized by Huttenlocher & Goodman, 1987, and others). Although lexical input is clearly essential for speech intelligibility, we cannot exclude the possibility that other, nonlexical, sources contribute to word identity. The process of word recognition predictably makes use of any information available in the context. For example, as many bisyllabic English words begin with a strong syllable followed by a weaker one, this pattern has been proposed as a useful clue for segmenting the sound stream (e.g., Cutler & Norris, 1988; Vroomen, van Zon, & de Gelder, 1996). However, we also have to remember the fact that about 64% of the words in written English are monosyllables and that only about 15% are polysyllabic words beginning with a strong syllable (calculated from Kučera & Francis, 1967). We might expect that word frequencies in spoken English will not differ much from these figures, forcing us to conclude that the localization of strong syllables may not play a significant role in the segmentation of sentences, and similar negative conclusions may apply to other simple rules. The fact that stress patterns differ between languages presents another objection to any type of fixed segmentation strategy.[3]

Additionally, we should not forget that spoken languages abound in phonetic ambiguities, such as the English *ice cream/I scream, what her/water, sweet tart/sweetheart*, and so on. Spencer and Wollman (1980), from whom these examples are taken, concluded that word familiarity and explicitly being told what will be presented, rather than contextual effects, were the main basis of their listeners' responses: "When listeners knew what they were supposed to hear, they usually heard it. When they did not know what they were to hear, they usually did not hear it" (p. 197). The authors cited a statement by R. A. Cole as an appropriate summary of the nature of speech perception: "In a sense, we recognize words by recreating the other person's train of thought; the speaker and listener share in the process of putting the speaker's thought into words" (p. 197).

Thus speech intelligibility is almost a paradox. As most words in fluent speech flow into and out of one another without clear boundaries, it seems that a word can be confidently recognized as a discrete part of the sentence only after the next word is also recognized. If this reasoning held strictly for each subsequent word, fluent speech would be unintelligible. Since this is not the case, uncertainties with respect to the successive words of a sentence must be overcome by the extra information represented by the listener's knowledge of the language.

There is an interesting analogue in reading aloud. It is impossible to read a text aloud in a fluent manner if the words are visually presented one at a time, just before they have to be pronounced. In order to pronounce the sentence with the right intonation and to locate the proper word accents, it is essential to see at least some of the following words, even if they are more peripherally than foveally presented and therefore less distinct. We need a moving visual "window" of several words for fluent reading. Similarly, the listening process seems to be characterized by a continuously moving *auditory window* of several words, in which some vagueness at the edges is allowed. As this analogy with reading has some interesting aspects, I return to it later.

---

[3]General reviews were published by Cole and Jakimik (1978), Cutler (1995), and Miller and Eimas (1995).

MENTAL LEXICON AND LEXICAL ACCESS

Recognition occurring as the combination of auditory as well as context-dependent cognitive processing makes use of an internal vocabulary. As mentioned in the previous chapter, it has been estimated that adults may know around 50,000 words. Linguists refer to this as the *mental lexicon*, the personal vocabulary we have at our disposal both for reception, in listening and reading, and for production, in speaking and writing.

However, there are large differences in how often we use the words we know, and word frequencies vary substantially between speaking and writing. This is beautifully illustrated by a comparison of words tabulated from personal discourse by H. Dahl (1979, published by Miller, 1991) and from written texts (Kučera & Francis, 1967), both collections comprising more than 1 million words. These counts indicate that conversation employs only about one-third of the words used in writing: 17,871 versus 50,406, respectively, in the two databases referred to. As Table 5.1 shows, there are even some characteristic differences in the frequency of the 20 most used words. It is remarkable that neither list contains a single noun. The table also illustrates that most frequently used words are short. This linguistic "efficiency" manifests itself still more strikingly in the cumulated frequency of the words in the two databases. The last row of the table indicates that the 20 words represent together 37% and 31% of the spoken and written words, respectively. Figure 5.8 gives the word frequency of the 1,000 most used words in written text as a function of their rank of occurrence, R. It is highly significant that the number of times a word is used is almost perfectly inversely proportional to its rank.[4] Moreover, it follows the very simple rule that the percentage of occurrence of any word is about equal to $1/10R$.

It would be most interesting to know how we manage to match within a few hundred milliseconds the acoustic form of a word to the listings in this huge mental lexicon. However, the "black box" of word recognition has not abandoned its secrets and it is possible that it never will. Extensive research of the last decades has shown that both semantic and phonetic relations play a role in the internal organization of the lexicon, but that is essentially all that can be said. I will discuss here a few generally accepted results on the recognition of spoken words, to be supplemented in the next section by findings on the recognition of written words. While these results support the view that words repre-

---

[4]This remarkable relationship was discovered and extensively studied by Zipf (1949/1965) as a general characteristic of languages as well as many other distributions. He considered it as manifesting a universal "principle of least effort."

sent the building blocks of speech, they still lift only a corner of the veil covering the mysterious process of how we understand speech.

A first important question is whether the large differences in familiarity are reflected in the quality of access to the lexicon: Are well-known words more easily recognized than rare words? Howes (1957) studied this question by investigating the intelligibility of spoken words as a function of their sound-pressure level relative to a background of electronically generated noise. He used small

TABLE 5.1

Frequency of the 20 Most Used Words in Personal Discourse (Miller, 1991) and Written Text (Kucera and Francis, 1967)

	Personal Discourse		Written Text	
	Word	%	Word	%
1	I	6.16	the	6.90
2	and	3.59	of	3.59
3	the	2.81	and	2.84
4	to	2.80	to	2.58
5	that	2.60	a	2.29
6	you	2.51	in	2.10
7	it	1.94	that	1.04
8	of	1.92	is	1.00
9	a	1.83	was	0.97
10	know	1.44	he	0.94
11	was	1.43	for	0.94
12	uh	1.32	it	0.86
13	in	1.22	with	0.72
14	but	0.93	as	0.71
15	is	0.84	his	0.69
16	this	0.83	on	0.66
17	me	0.80	be	0.63
18	about	0.79	at	0.53
19	just	0.79	by	0.52
20	don't	0.78	I	0.51
Sum		37.34		31.04

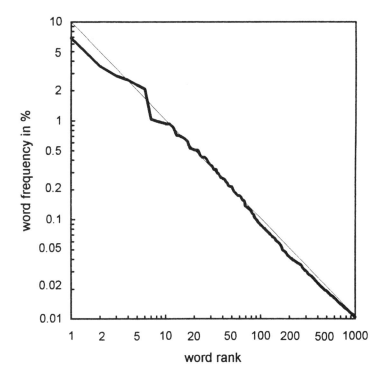

FIG. 5.8.   Word frequency of the 1000 most used words in written text as a function of their
rank of occurrence (based on data from Kučera & Francis, 1967).

sets of words consisting of a fixed number of letters, varying from 1 to 21, and
differing over a wide range in their frequency of occurrence in written texts. As
the number of letters in a word is not the best predictor of its intelligibility, I calculated the overall speech-to-noise ratio for 50% correct intelligibility score for
his words with one to nine letters. The results are plotted in Fig. 5.9 as a function
of their frequency in the database. As the critical speech-to-noise ratio may be
accepted as a reliable measure of word familiarity, we can conclude that the
probability of recognizing a word increases monotonically with its frequency of
use in the language.

   However, word recognition depends not only on familiarity. It seems reasonable that a word "surrounded" by phonetically similar words will be confused
more easily than a word without such neighbors. Luce and Pisoni (1998) studied this question for 811 consonant–vowel–consonant meaningful words by
comparing the phonetic transcription of the target word with all other phonetic
descriptions. As a result, each word could be represented by a number express-

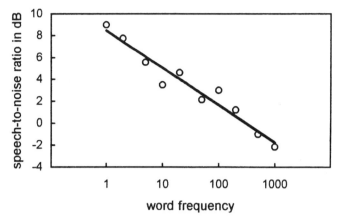

FIG. 5.9.   Speech-to-noise ratio for 50% correct identification of words as a function of their frequency in written texts (based on data from Howes, 1957).

ing its relative probability of being confused with other words. Listening tests in which the words were presented against a background of noise confirmed the hypothesis. The highest recognition scores were obtained for the most familiar, least confusable words. The lowest scores, on the other hand, were found for the least familiar, most confusable words. These results demonstrate how well the decision strategy of word recognition makes use of all information available to arrive at the most likely solution.

Many attempts to penetrate deeper into the process of word recognition have employed reaction times. Savin and Bever (1970) measured the time required to identify either the initial consonant of a syllable or the entire syllable. Listeners were presented with lists of nonsense syllables. On half of the trials they had to press a button as soon as they heard a syllable beginning with /b/ or /s/, and in the other half as soon as they heard a particular syllable (e.g., /bæb/). Reaction times were significantly shorter for identifying entire syllables than their initial phonemes, and the authors concluded that phoneme identification occurs subsequent to the perception of larger phonological units. They went so far as to say:

> Having perceived the syllable, why not always proceed directly to morphemes, phrases, and other semantically relevant units? This question immediately raises the further one: what is the evidence that people normally *do* (outside of experiments like ours and grade-school reading classes) bother with the seemingly superfluous analysis of syllables into phonemes? (p. 300)

Of course, such openly expressed disrespect for the phoneme as the basic unit in speech perception was not received with equanimity by many of their colleagues, and led to a series of subsequent studies.[5] Segui, Frauenfelder, and Mehler (1981) refined the conclusion by showing that only the following vowel is sufficient for identification of the initial consonant. This means that the mental lexicon may not always be involved, and brings us back to our discussion in the previous chapter on the contribution of spelling knowledge to phoneme identification. The listener needs to hear the next vowel to know how to "spell" the preceding consonant, and this takes extra time.

THE ROLE OF CONTEXT IN READING

As there is such a close relation between the spoken and the written word, it is instructive at this point, as in the previous chapter, to take note of some reading studies. This is all the more true in view of the fact that these studies were undertaken much earlier than comparable intelligibility experiments. Visual reading investigations began more than a century ago with the work of the highly talented James McKeen Cattell (1860–1944).[6] Cattell left America after his graduation in 1880 to attend lectures in Leipzig given by Wilhelm Wundt (1832–1920), the famous founder of experimental psychology, and in Göttingen by Rudolph Lotze (1817–1881). Cattell became quite enthusiastic about Wundt's approach, and undertook a series of reaction-time experiments that brought him back to Leipzig again. Here he published his first paper (Cattell, 1885) reporting many important results on the minimal exposure time required to read letters, words, and sentences. Rather than reviewing this work in my own words, I cite here from Huey's (1908/1968) excellent early summary of results obtained by Cattell and others. After explaining that the eyes scan the printed text in steps with pauses in which 20–30 letters may be captured, suggesting that "reading must go on by some other means than the recognition of letter after letter as was once supposed," Huey wrote:

> Professor Cattell early concluded, as a result of his experiments at Leipsic upon the amount which could be read in single short exposures, that we read in word-wholes and even, sometimes, in phrase and sentence wholes, and not by letters. This was evidently before the nature of the eye's movement was known to him, although the discontinuous character of the movement had already been determined by Professor Javal and his pupils. Cattell found that when single words were momentarily exposed, they were recognized as quickly as single letters, and indeed that it took longer to name letters than to name whole words, the exposures being made under conditions in which the times could be accurately measured.

---

[5]For a discussion, see Mehler, Segui, and Frauenfelder (1981).
[6]In 1888, Cattell became the world's first professor of psychology, and in 1894 he was cofounder of *Psychological Review* and publisher of *Science*. More biographical data can be found in Poffenberger (1947).

It was found that when sentences or phrases were exposed, they were either grasped as wholes or else scarcely any of the words or letters were read. This observation was strikingly confirmed in the writer's experiments in which sentences were momentarily exposed. Rarely were single letters read, even as forming the beginning or ends of words that were but partially recognized. The readings were of whole words, and almost always of words connected in some sense fashion. (pp. 72–73)

Huey also pointed to the fact that words with their letters written in a vertical line are much more difficult to read than when the letters are ordered horizontally from left to right as usual. He concluded:

Why should not a familiar word-form be recognized and named on sight just as a house or wall is recognized and named? We do not, in the latter cases, take account of the constituent stories and bricks; nor of all the sticks and limbs and leaves in recognizing a particular thicket or oak tree. The arrangement, the total form, is the main thing, whether in the recognition of letters, numbers, words, or objects of whatsoever sort. (p. 75)

These comments sound as if they were recently written. They are important in more than one respect. It is revealing to discover that more than a century ago scientists were able to apply tachistoscopic techniques still popular today. The text cited here contains not only excellent *avant la lettre* formulations of a basic gestalt principle, but also an experimental verification, more than can be said of most early work in that field. In his description of the perception of a "visual whole," Huey used the terms *arrangement* and *parts*, still considered to be the best terms (e.g., Uttal, 1988).

It is highly remarkable that half a century before the phoneme was launched as the basic unit in speech perception, the grapheme as its visual counterpart was, on experimental grounds, already firmly rejected as the basic unit in reading. This is the more surprising as the independence of graphemes is obvious whereas the independence of phonemes is not.

It took nearly half a century before word reading received new attention, this time, again, as a result of quite surprising observations. In 1935, Stroop published the results of what has since come to be considered a classic experiment. He presented his subjects with a list of color names printed in color and found that they could name the colors of the words much more quickly if the color of the print agreed with the color name represented by the word than if it did not. This so-called *Stroop effect* indicates that the subjects, although requested *not* to read the words, could not avoid this, resulting in response retardation and errors. The effect demonstrates nicely the "automatic" tendency to see and read words as unities. Experiments have also confirmed that words are read more quickly when they are more familiar.

The priority of words over letters was additionally verified in a quite different approach by G. M. Reicher (communicated by Miller, 1991). He presented his subjects with visual stimuli such as "HEAR" and "AEHR" and asked them to report whether the final letter was D or R. Accuracy was significantly better for meaningful words than for nonsense words. Apparently, the subjects could not avoid reading the entire word in responding to the question. Wheeler (1970) extended this experiment by comparing reaction times required for recognizing individual letters and words. He concluded:

> Performance on words was consistently better than on single letters in all cases.... It seems appropriate to stop trying to explain away the phenomenon and, instead, to consider the implications for models of the human recognition system.
>
> The major conclusion to be drawn from the strength and persistence of the word superiority effect ... is that word recognition cannot be analyzed into a set of independent letter recognition processes. There is an interaction among the letters such that the context of the other letters of a meaningful word improves recognition despite the control of letter redundancy. (p. 78)

These experiments demonstrate that there is an irresistible inclination to see familiar words as perceptual wholes rather than as strings of letters. We have noted in the previous chapter that learning the individual letters is an essential part of learning to read. We have to know the letters in order to extend our vocabulary. The reader will need the letter mode to discover that MCMXCVI in Roman numerals represents the same year as 1996 in Arabic numerals. However, as soon as we are familiar with the "pictures" of words, particularly the frequent ones, we grasp them as unities. This is the most efficient way of reading. Kolers (1972) pointed out that if a reader had to see every letter one by one in order to read a word, reading rate would be limited to roughly 35 words per minute, whereas good readers can go as fast as 300 words per minute.

The year 1996 when written in Roman numerals also demonstrates that the assumption of independence in reading letters of the written language is not as rigid as it might seem to be. We can evaluate the first C only in combination with the following M, the X only in combination with the following C. Mutual dependencies occur particularly in languages with substantial deviations from the ideal phoneme–grapheme congruence, as is the case for English. For example, in the word *phone* we need the *h* to know that the sound of the initial consonant is /f/, not /p/, and we need the *e* to know that the vowel is /o/, not /ɔ/, and to recognize the additional peculiarity that the final *e* is not pronounced. These ambiguities are so numerous in English that foreigners (and apparently many native speakers, too!) learning to read English need the phonetic transcriptions of the dictionary to tell how the words are pronounced.

The role of eye movements in reading has recently been extensively studied. As the quotation from Huey showed, the fact that the eye jumps (makes "saccades") during reading from one fixed point to the next, rather than moving continuously, was already known in the beginning of the 20th century. These saccades correspond in normal reading with a span of about seven letters, with a standard deviation of three letters (for a review, see O'Regan, 1990). This means that, on the average, our eyes move from word to word. The average duration of the successive fixations is 200–250 msec. It is clear that reading would be greatly delayed if our vision were restricted to the text segment covered only by the fovea, the area of sharpest vision.

Rayner and Bertera (1979) investigated the reading rate of sentences as a function of the number of letters (including spaces) simultaneously presented to the reader. They used a computer-controlled cathode-ray tube that presented an adjustable number of letters around the fixation point of the eyes, to be called the *window*; the more remote letters were masked. The window jumped synchronously with the monitored eye movements. The curve in Fig. 5.10 shows that reading rate increased rapidly with the width of the window, up to an asymptote of about 30 letters. This indicates that remote letters, as many as 14 to the right of fixation, although only vaguely seen, still contribute to word recognition in reading.[7]

An interesting question is whether the access code employed in reading is purely visual or whether a first conversion into speech is involved. In other words: Is reading an achievement on its own or is it actually silent speaking? Children learn to read by pronouncing words in order to grasp the correspondence between phonemes and graphemes. Is this only an aid to the teacher for evaluation and correction, or is it an essential stage of the process, which continues subliminally in silent reading?

This question has concerned many investigators. By introspection, it may appear that we have the experience of pronouncing silently words we read. But this does not mean that the phonological route is necessary. Just as we see and interpret our surroundings directly, whether the furniture in a room or the traffic in the street, without any speech involvement, it is possible that we are able to see and grasp the meaning of written words and sentences without actually saying them. Moreover, the reading rate of a skilled reader can be so high, and his or her scanning of the text may be so haphazard, that the process may differ fundamentally from listening to a speaker. Experiments designed to address the

---

[7]For the identification of parafoveally presented letters, see O'Regan, Lévy-Schoen, and Jacobs (1983).

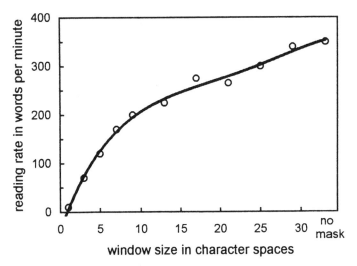

FIG. 5.10.   Reading rate of text as a function of window size (based on data from Rayner &
Bertera, 1979).

question certainly have not led to unequivocal conclusions (cf. Besner, 1987;
Downing & Leong, 1982). One gets the impression that the answer strongly depends on the experimental task involved. The divergence of conclusions based
on different experimental approaches to the same question suggests that there
is no one perceptual strategy. Probably, the visual route exists in addition to the
phonological route, and the reading process can use both depending on the required efficiency. The opposite case, considering whether we have to spell
words in order to understand them, is more easily answered because being able
to read is not essential for speech comprehension. Nevertheless, literate speakers and listeners like to know how words are spelled, and, as we have seen, spelling may play an essential and almost automatic role in word-recognition
experiments using listeners who are also trained in reading.

We have already mentioned the contrast between the "continuity" of words
in speech and the clear divisions between words in written language. The "co-
hesion" of the phonemes constituting a spoken word is much greater—one
might say much more basic—than of the letters in a written word. However, we
should not forget that written text contains ambiguities that are not present in
the spoken version. For instance, in the printed sentence "wearetrainingateam"
the string segments "wear," "rain," and "gate" can be recognized first and keep
us from decoding the sentence, "we are training a team," whereas such uncertainties are entirely absent if we hear the sentence pronounced.

THE EFFECTS OF DISTURBING NOISE

In the previous chapter and in this chapter, we have reviewed studies using "clean" speech. However, this is not enough. For two reasons, we must consider the situation where the speech signal is disturbed by other simultaneous sounds, ranging from interfering noises to competing voices. First, listening to speech in quiet is the exception rather than the rule, and even then, a listener can speak at the same time as another speaker without missing what has been said. Speech perception against a background of other sounds is the normal listening condition, and listeners are remarkably able to cope with this situation.

The second reason follows directly from the first. If retrieving speech out of a mixture of unrelated sounds is such an easy task, this must mean that the hearing process is especially "designed" to do it, and we must consider its implications for the theory of speech perception. This holds all the more since concepts derived from experiments using uninterrupted speech may not be able to explain intelligibility for cases where speech segments are partially or fully masked. Speech scientists are traditionally accustomed to studying speech under what they consider to be optimal conditions, excluding noise and other disturbing factors, yet the test case for any theory of speech perception is speech comprehension under everyday, realistic listening conditions.

In discussing the perception of multiple sounds in chapter 3, we saw that when speech is periodically alternated with noise bursts of, say, 100 msec, it sounds as if the speech were continuously present, all through the noise. Figure 3.11 showed that words interrupted in this way remain quite intelligible. Apparently, our auditory system is provided with processes that can restore the speech signal on the basis of context. Warren's (1970) experiment demonstrated that when listeners are presented with a word in which a phoneme is replaced by a short cough sound, they are convinced they heard the complete word and, moreover, are unable to tell which phoneme was actually missing. Now we need to consider the implications of this phenomenon for the intelligibility of fluent speech as well as its relevance for theories of speech perception in general.

Regular, periodic interruptions of the speech signal are rather exceptional in daily life. A much more common situation is that the weaker parts of the speech signal are masked by noise. This type of listening condition has been investigated extensively and some principal results follow. In the first place, it is important to know that intelligibility scores depend over a large range exclusively on speech-to-noise ratio. This means that if we increase the noise level by 10 dB, we also have to increase the speech level by 10 dB in order to maintain intelligibility at the same level. This relationship reveals that the ear's behavior in this respect is comparable to a linear system. The speech-to-noise ratio for which

50% of recorded sentences are repeated correctly by listeners, the so-called *speech-reception threshold* (SRT), is a reliable measure to compare different conditions. Figure 5.11 shows how SRTs for 50 listeners varied with noise level (Duquesnoy & Plomp, 1983). The horizontal asymptote represents the absolute hearing threshold. The best-fit theoretical curve is based on the assumption that absolute threshold is the result of a constant internal noise added to the external noise.

The relation between intelligibility score and speech-to-noise ratio is plotted in Fig. 5.12. The solid curve gives the average percentage of correctly repeated sentences presented against a background of speechlike noise (Festen & Plomp, 1990). The change from a speech-to-noise ratio of –8 dB to –2 dB was sufficient to increase the intelligibility score from 10% to 90%. The sentences were completely intelligible in noise that was at the same level as the speech (speech-to-noise ratio 0 dB). If we combine this with the fact that the peaks of the speech signal exceed the long-term average value by about 10 dB, we can conclude that the upper 10-dB range of the speech signal is sufficient for understanding fluent speech. This is a remarkably small range compared with the full range of variations of more than 30 dB covered by the speech signal overall.

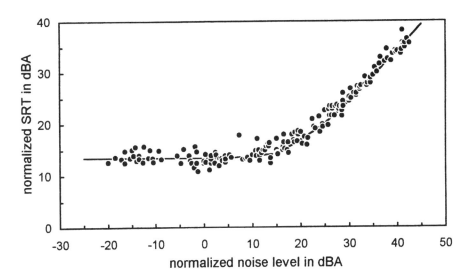

FIG. 5.11.   Individual speech-reception thresholds of sentences in noise for 50 listeners as a function of noise level. The data from each subject were normalized by the theoretical curve based on the assumption that the speech-reception threshold is determined exclusively by the speech-to-noise ratio, with the absolute threshold as internal noise (redrawn from Duquesnoy & Plomp, 1983).

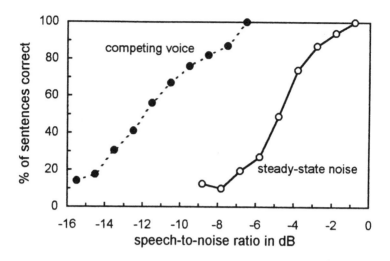

FIG. 5.12.   Correct intelligibility score for sentences as a function of speech-to-noise ratio, with steady-state noise or a competing voice as the noise (redrawn from Festen & Plomp, 1990).

The solid curve in Fig. 5.12 is for adults listening to sentences in their native language. Such individuals owe their ability to understand speech presented in such high levels of noise to their familiarity with the language. In contrast, children, with less linguistic experience, require a significantly higher speech-to-noise ratio to achieve comparable scores (Elliott, 1979). Informal tests with foreign students presented with sentences in their second language indicated that their lack of experience expressed itself in a 4-dB higher speech-reception threshold.

Our ability to understand speech in spite of noise is even more striking in the common everyday condition where the source of interference is a competing speaker rather than steady-state noise. The dashed curve in Fig. 5.12 represents this condition. The curve indicates that an approximately 7 dB lower speech-to-noise ratio can be tolerated in this condition as compared to steady-state noise. In this case, sentences appear to be fully intelligible at a level more than 6 dB lower than the competing voice. In practice, this means that we are able to follow a speaker who is twice as far away as the interfering speaker (sound reflections excluded). These values are for monaural listening without visual information. When lipreading is available, at least another 4 dB may be added (Middelweerd & Plomp, 1987).

An often overlooked test case of listeners' excellent performance with respect to speech intelligibility is the common occurrence where the listener interrupts the speaker. It would be highly annoying if our own voice would make the speaker's voice unintelligible. However, for typical distances up to 1 or 2 m, such interruptions are no problem.

The considerable gain associated with a single interfering voice compared to steady-state noise (such as the voice babble of many speakers) can be explained by the fact that both the interfering signal and the target signal vary continuously in time. This means that the amount of masking changes from moment to moment such that fragments of even weak phonemes have a chance to be heard, which is not possible with steady-state noise. One can remove all parts of an interfering speech signal (measured through ¼ octave bands) that exceed the target speech signal in level, and yet the target sentences will remain remarkably intelligible.

Another significant gain is provided by binaural hearing. We noted in chapter 3 that the speech-reception threshold of sentences in the presence of a single noise source can be improved by as much as 10 dB by increasing the difference in apparent direction of the two sounds. As can be expected, this benefit of binaural hearing will be diminished in the case of multiple noise sources. Binaural advantage in this condition (the *cocktail-party effect*) has been estimated to be about 3 dB (Bronkhorst & Plomp, 1992).

In addition to speech intelligibility, the perception process is called on to decide which fragments belong to which voice. Attempts to simulate this task technologically confirm that this ability is indeed an extraordinary achievement. However, as we know from experience, it is accomplished so effortlessly that we are inclined to overlook the degree of difficulty involved. Even 7.5-month-old infants show signs of being able to separate simultaneous sounds to some extent (Newman & Jusczyk, 1996).

It appears to be much more difficult to separate sentences pronounced by the same speaker than sentences pronounced by different speakers. This indicates that speaker-specific differences in pitch and timbre, as well as timing cues, provide the bases for separating voices into streams (e.g., Darwin, 1984; Nooteboom, Brokx, & de Rooij, 1976). The process seems so natural that it has been greatly underestimated scientifically. Although the separation of voices manifests itself as an "automatic" process, equally effective for speech as well as other sounds, it should be seen as an important stage preceding interpretation.

The dependence of sentence intelligibility on speech-to-noise ratio illustrates the role of context in the recognition of fluent speech. One early illustration is an experiment reported by Miller and Isard (1963) in which they tested the intelligibility of sentences consisting of six words but differing semantically and linguistically, as in the following examples:

Grammatical: *trains carry passengers across the country.*

Anomalous: *trains steal elephants around the highway.*
Ungrammatical: *around accidents country honey the shoot.*
Figure 5.13 presents the percentage of such sentences correctly repeated by the listeners. The curves differ substantially. Whereas more than 60% of the grammatically correct sentences could be accurately repeated at 0 dB speech-to-noise ratio, this score was not even approached for the ungrammatical sentences presented in the absence of noise. The data plotted in Fig. 5.5 offer another example of how context contributes to the recognition of words presented in noise.

It is interesting to compare again listening with reading, in this case, the effect of interruptions on the intelligibility of spoken versus written texts. Miller and Friedman (1957) presented their readers with texts consisting of 300 characters, where some letters were replaced by underlined blanks (to distinguish deleted letters from spaces between words). The readers were allowed 10 min to reconstruct the text. The solid curve in Fig. 5.14 represents the average percentage of correctly reconstructed characters as a function of the percentage of characters (letters plus spaces) removed. The dashed curve gives intelligibility scores, derived from data by Miller and Licklider (1950), for spoken words interrupted by silent intervals of about the same lengths as the phonemes. Although there are substantial physical differences between the two conditions, performance in the two experiments differs to such an extent that we may conclude that interruptions seem to be much more disastrous for written than for spoken language. If phoneme identification were a prerequisite of speech perception,

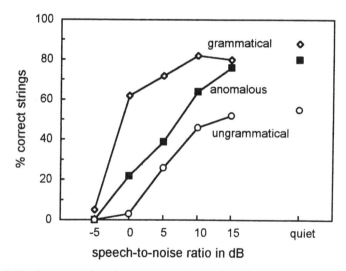

FIG. 5.13.   Percentage of word strings repeated correctly by the listeners as a function of speech-to-noise ratio (redrawn from Miller & Isard, 1963).

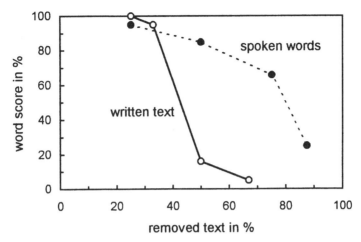

FIG. 5.14.   The solid curve represents the percentage of characters correctly reconstructed from a printed text as a function of the percentage of periodically removed characters (based on data from Miller & Friedman, 1957), the dashed curve the intelligibility score for spoken words interrupted periodically by silent intervals of about the same length as phonemes (based on data from Miller & Licklider, 1950).

one would expect much more comparable scores. These findings support the view that word recognition in reading depends on much more elementalistic processes than in listening. Figure 5.15 illustrates how difficult it is to read a text of which 50% is masked, a condition under which nearly all words of a spoken text can be easily recognized.

This leads us to the question of the theoretical impact of the findings reviewed here. Context contributes so considerably to the intelligibility of speech disturbed by other sounds that established theories focusing on phonemes or words fall far short of a satisfactory explanation regarding how fluent speech is actually perceived. The great tolerance for masking or the elimination of seemingly essential elements or properties of the speech signal indicates that no one element is indispensable. Apparently, holistic rather than elementalistic aspects dominate the speech perception process.

DISCUSSION

We have seen in this chapter that fluent speech is characterized by enormous redundancy. Spectrotemporal variations are the basis of speech intelligibility, but they contain much more information than seems to be required in speech communication. This surplus of information is not accounted for by easy identification of the individual phonemes, but depends on the recognition of familiar

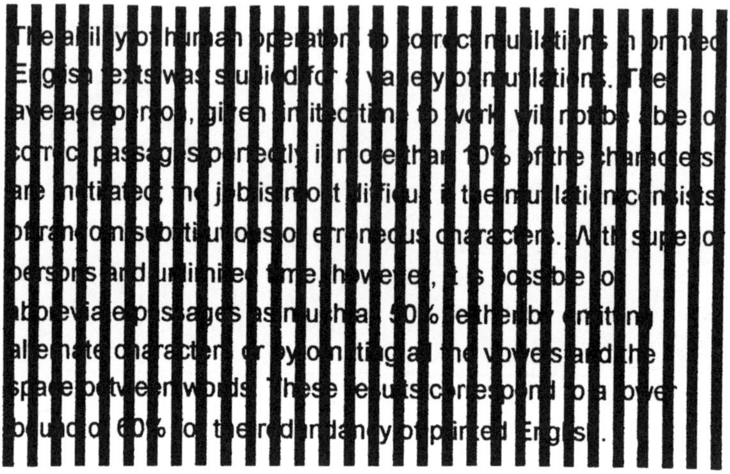

FIG. 5.15. Abstract of Miller and Friedman's (1957) paper with about 50% of the text masked by bars roughly a single character wide.

words and the contribution of acoustic, linguistic, and semantic context. As a result, speech is surprisingly resistant to large differences in pronunciation, substantial deficiencies in the faithfulness of the transmission to the ear of the listener, and severe competition by interfering sounds.

Of course, we owe the redundancy of speech in the first place to the superb performance of the auditory system. Speech in everyday situations would be much more difficult to understand if the ear's critical bands, the basis of its frequency resolution, were wider than they actually are. Many hearing-impaired people complain about being unable to converse in a noisy place such as a cocktail party. It has been found that their auditory frequency-resolving power has deteriorated. A doubling of the critical bandwidth, roughly requiring a 3-dB higher speech-to-noise ratio, appears to represent a substantial handicap (Plomp, 1986). This demonstrates that the noise conditions accepted in daily life are actually at the limits of what normally hearing people can tolerate. Even a relatively small deterioration from this can render speech unintelligible in environments that would otherwise be acceptable for most people. Reductions in the ear's temporal resolution, although less common, can result in similar difficulties.

Although the purely auditory components of perception are important for listening to speech, by far the greatest contribution to the ear's flexibility in speech perception is of a cognitive nature. Many cognitive factors determine our ability to understand what has been said. Of course, most essential is our familiarity with the language spoken. From the first days of life, we receive intensive training in the meaning of speech sounds, which differences in pronunciation are significant, how words are combined into sentences, and so on. As a result, as we have seen in this chapter, very serious disturbances in the speech signal as well as interference from strong disturbing sounds can be introduced, and speech still remains intelligible.

This flexibility makes it almost impossible to formulate the speech-perception process in terms of a well-defined theory. As discussed in the preceding chapter, there has been a strong tendency up to now to consider the phoneme as the basic perceptual unit. The spectral differences made visible in the spectrogram were interpreted as including enough unique information to identify the various speech sounds, either directly, or more indirectly as references to their underlying articulatory gestures (the motor theory of speech perception). In particular, the vowels have been traditionally seen as characterized consistently by their formant structure, and many studies have been conducted to investigate various properties of this structure, such as the interindividual spread and systematic differences between men, women, and children.

In view of the intelligibility of fluent speech maintained under widely differing conditions, we can rightly question many statements regarding the basic role of phonemes in speech perception. The low identification scores obtained by Shockey and Reddy (1975) for phonemes in texts spoken in a foreign language, and by Koopmans-van Beinum (1980) for vowels extracted from free conversation, demonstrate that if we had no sources other than phoneme fragments at our disposal, speech perception would be almost impossible. Moreover, wide-band spectral smearing and sharp filtering appear to be tolerated, although both seriously perturb spectral structure. Masking of individual phonemes by noise scarcely affects the intelligibility of sentences as a whole. As we have seen, listeners may not even be aware of missing phonemes. These examples are sufficient to demonstrate that the role of the individual phonemes as elements in speech perception is rather modest. This holds also for (meaningless) combinations of consonants and vowels. From the evidence presented in this chapter, we may conclude that the tentative rejection of the basic role of phonemes in speech perception outlined in the preceding chapter was justified.

It is amazing to consider the extent to which speech perception research has focused on the identification of single phonemes rather than the perception of speech as a whole. It is not difficult to collect hundreds of papers and book chapters discussing phonemes, whether vowels or consonants, with not a single reference to the cognitive aspects of speech perception. Two recent examples illustrate the point. Rosner and Pickering (1994) published an important volume on the perception and production of vowels without acknowledging the large spread of the vowel spectra in fluent speech and the rather modest relevance of spectral peaks for intelligibility. With respect to consonants, it is of interest to mention the valuable collection of reprinted articles Liberman (1996) published under the title *Speech: A Special Code*. Liberman added a first chapter surveying his arguments in favor of the motor theory of speech perception without including any discussion of how these arguments stand up against descriptions of cognitive processes such as those discussed in this chapter.

If phonemes have to be dismissed, the next step would be to consider meaningful words as possible candidates for the basic units in speech perception.[8] Without doubt, this is a substantial improvement compared with phonemes. The recognition of individual words does represent an essential and major stage in language acquisition, in particular for infants and for adults learning a second language. However, we have also seen that the intelligibility of words depends in turn on their context. Of course, the meaning of words provides the basis for understanding a sentence, but, at the same time, grasping the entire sentence appears to be important for correct recognition of individual words. Similarly, as a word is more than the sum of phonemes, a sentence is more than the sum of words. In view of this fact, attempts to base speech perception exclusively on the successive recognition of words in a linear order, as outlined for example in Norris's (1994) recent "shortlist" model, are unsatisfactory.

The inevitable conclusion seems to be that speech perception is a holistic rather than an elementalistic process, starting from sentences or parts of sentences covering perhaps at least 1 sec of speech. Although this conclusion seems to describe much of the data, this one-sentence statement still cannot comprehend all aspects of speech perception. The success of speech perception at the sentence level presupposes that we are familiar with all the words and therefore that we have no difficulty segmenting the continuous speech stream. However, the reality is more complex. An unfamiliar word appearing in the sentence may disturb the process by drawing the listener's attention away from the whole to that particular word. The listener may have to ask for its meaning before being able to understand the sentence as a whole. In the case of an unknown name, the listener may want the name repeated or even spelled. Moreover, there are large differences among languages that can affect perceptual strategy. This is readily illustrated in reading where similar problems can

---

[8]I do not consider Fowler's theory of listeners as realistic perceivers to be a serious alternative (e.g., Fowler, 1987).

arise with the whole and the elements. The English language is characterized by compound words as *world war* using a space between the component parts. The German language represents the extreme opposite in which long words as *Vermögenszuwachssteuergesetzentwurf* (not invented by the author!), composed of the five nouns *Vermögen, Zuwachs, Steuer, Gesetz,* and *Entwurf,* are not uncommon. It is clear that such differences can play a role in the perception process. The English reader has less need to segment words than the German reader has.

The moral of these considerations is that the great flexibility of the speech-perception process makes it impossible to summarize it in a simplistic model. We cannot formulate a rigid framework describing how we arrive at intelligible speech that holds for all conditions. We know reasonably well the factors involved, but the actual roles they play in each particular case depends on the listener's familiarity with the language, expectations, the specific content of the message, the listening conditions, and so on. It is most remarkable that, although the acoustic information concerning the elemental speech sounds may be quite fragmentary or even absent, the listener is usually convinced that all words were heard perfectly well.

CONCLUSIONS

In the preceding chapter we concluded that words rather than phonemes represent the best candidates for the perceptual units of speech. This conclusion betrayed the influence of an inclination to view the perception of fluent speech as a linear process based on perceiving a sequence of words one after another.

The present chapter reviewed evidence that the perception of fluent speech is actually governed by much more complex principles. Just as the identification of consonants appears to depend on the preceding and following vowels, the recognition of spoken words depends on the context of the sentence as a whole. For example, we found that words can be unintelligible in isolation but perfectly well recognized in sentences. The role of the context is so great that we concluded it is appropriate to conceptualize speech perception as a holistic rather than an elementalistic process.

However, the reality of listening is still too complex for such a short formulation. As long as the listener is presented with more or less "routine" speech, perception can be satisfactorily explained as a holistic process in which context plays a dominant role. But the situation can be quite different if the subject is not familiar with the speech being listened to. For example, a child or a second-language student may stumble over a single unknown word, which has to be explained before the sentence can be understood. On these and many other occasions, the listener may need to fall back on a much more elementalistic approach. Hence, the conditions of speech perception are too divergent for us to formulate a uniform strategy for listening that will be appropriate in all situations.

6
Hearing Research in Perspective

We have seen in the preceding chapters that hearing is a very complex process. The successive chapters showed progressively the many aspects involved, ranging from the ear's frequency analysis as an auditory mechanism to the role of context in listening to fluent speech as a cognitive process.

In this final chapter, I discuss some main points important for our understanding of the prominent characteristics of the sound-perception process with respect to the task it has to perform. Hearing is preeminently the instrument by which we communicate with the outside world in general and with other human beings in particular. The transfer of information can be effective only if the receiver is familiar with the code hidden in the sounds. On the street this means that we need to know not only the direction and composition of a sound, but also whether it stands for a barking dog or an oncoming car. In the concert hall, sounds are recognized as produced by certain musical instruments and form a pattern we may be familiar with. In many cases, the sounds represent a spoken message directed to us and we are supposed to understand the message and to respond to it. In all these examples, our hearing draws on the arsenal of earlier experiences in order to perceive the sounds adequately.

To place the findings discussed in previous chapters in the proper perspective, it may be worthwhile to start by reconsidering the role of the four characteristics of past hearing research mentioned in chapter 1. In that chapter, I explained their importance more generally, and now we can examine their specific roles in the study of sound perception.

FOUR TYPES OF BIAS

In the introduction, the following four types of bias characterizing the way in which sound perception has been studied in the past were discussed: (a) the dominance of sinusoidal tones, (b) the predilection for a "microscopic" approach, (c) the preference for the psychophysical aspects of perception, and (d) the abstraction from "dirty" everyday conditions. These points were merely discussed in general terms. After our tour of the main topics of the perceptual process, we are better able to consider the actual role they have played, consciously or unconsciously, in hearing research. As the four preferences are correlated to some degree, I have selected the examples in such a way that the specific role of each may become more apparent.

Bias 1: Sinusoidal Tones

Perhaps the most striking characteristic of hearing research for a long period was the almost exclusive use of sinusoidal stimuli. As was acknowledged in chapter 1, this preference has contributed considerably to our understanding of hearing, but, nevertheless, it should be seen as a rather biased view. Without doubt, it took its origin from the successful application of Fourier's well-known theorem in physics. The transmission of linear vibrations could be fully described by means of sinusoids, suggesting that sinusoids should be an extremely useful tool for the study of hearing. Developments in electronics for sound transmission confirmed the basic utility of the sinusoid. Both the theory and the design of even the most complicated analog circuit depend on how sinusoidal currents are transmitted. Hence, it seemed natural to apply the same approach to the study of tone perception, and to accept the sinusoidal tone as the element best able to explain relations between sounds presented to the ear and the corresponding sensations. However, this reduction of tone perception to a purely linear physical process, in which the whole can be described as the sum of the parts, came with a price. It led the sciences of auditory perception astray and substantially delayed our progress toward understanding. Two examples may illustrate the point.

The first concerns the perception of pitch, the core of any hearing theory. As shown in chapter 2, Helmholtz's view that the pitch of a tone is based on its fundamental was almost generally accepted up to the middle of the 20th century. In fact, this concept acknowledged that most real-world tones contain a number of harmonics, but the role of the lowest partial was considered to be so dominant that, with respect to pitch, any tone could be fairly represented by a sinusoidal vibration. It appeared rather difficult to depart from this traditional view, to suggest that *not* the fundamental but a series of resolved harmonics determines pitch.

As a second example, I take the attribute of timbre, usually defined negatively (and embarrassingly) as the quality of a tone left when pitch and loudness are separated out. Whereas Helmholtz discussed timbre extensively as an attribute of harmonic composition, attention directed mainly to single sinusoidal tones meant that timbre was almost completely neglected for a long time. Only more recently has timbre received proper attention as a major attribute of sounds. Modern techniques for sound recording, production, and testing paved the way for a rebirth of timbre research, reviewed briefly in chapter 2. It has become abundantly clear that the timbre of a complex tone cannot be seen simply as the sum of the timbres of its sinusoidal components.

Sinusoids determined by only two variables, amplitude and frequency, were also attractive for other reasons. Their use was in keeping with the traditional ideal of research to have experimental setups as simple as possible. This brings us to the second type of bias.

Bias 2: The Microscopic Approach

This term refers to the scientific tradition that prefers studying small manageable subcomponents rather than larger systems. Such an approach certainly can boast of countless impressive successes, but it has also its blind spots. It can result in a rather one-sided, or even wrong, picture of the processes involved in a system as a whole.

The preceding chapters have presented several examples of the microscopic approach, sometimes with excellent but in other cases with rather doubtful results. In chapter 2 we saw several impressive positive examples of its power. Experiments using well-defined sinusoidal tones are very appropriate for specifying the ear's frequency-analyzing power. The resulting masking curves give an excellent picture of the extent to which simultaneous sounds are individually audible. More generally, the microscopic approach has been ideal for understanding the mechanical and hydrodynamical transmission of sound in the peripheral ear, the excitation of action potentials in the hair cells, and their propagation along the nerve fibers to higher centers.

But this approach has been much less satisfying for studying the perception of successive sounds, as discussed in chapter 3. This may explain why the continuity effect and stream segregation of tone sequences, both quite fundamental qualities of auditory perception, did not receive appropriate attention until quite recently. Consequently, their role in hearing has been greatly neglected.

As the speech signal is a rather complex sound, with highly essential dynamical aspects, it is not surprising that the deficiencies of a too one-sided microscopic approach are particularly manifest in this field of study. It seems to me that the familiarity with written language as a string of discrete letters has dominated speech-perception research in the past, and still does. Nothing was more attractive for the microscopic observer than to conceptualize the existence of an alphabet of phonemes and to study them as characteristic elements of speech. Many phoneticians have modeled themselves on the ideal microscopic observer.

However, this behavior has profound risks. In the first place, as shown in chapter 4, the growing insight that the awareness of phonemes is the result of training in spelling struck a severe blow to the phoneme's position. Word perception appears to be much better explained as a form of *pattern recognition* than as the result of identifying strings of more or less discrete phonemes. Moreover, chapter 5 showed that this recognition peculiarity is not restricted to words but effectively extends over much larger portions of speech. It seems to me that the macroscopic point of view has gained ground primarily in response to problems encountered in developing reliable automatic speech recognizers. It has also been given fresh impetus from linguistics, presaged by Bagley's (1900–1901) prescient comments. However, the symbiotic joining of the microscopic and the macroscopic approaches is yet to come.

Bias 3: Psychophysical Aspects

The recognition of the macroscopic approach as an essential complement of the microscopic approach does not automatically mean that sound perception as a whole is seen in the proper light. One may be convinced that words are perceived as patterns, but this can still be interpreted as a purely psychophysical phenomenon. It rises beyond that level as soon as one begins to realize that sound perception is more than auditory sensation. Sounds are significant as carriers of information. They inform the listener about happenings in the outside world in general, and about the thoughts a speaker is attempting to communicate in particular. Sounds have meaning, implying that their significance is much greater than the physical content of the signal.

This essential aspect of sound as a carrier of information has long been underestimated, often even neglected, in hearing research. Most early textbooks dealt exclusively with the psychophysical aspects of hearing. If a chapter on speech was included, the discussion was usually limited to an explanation of the spectrogram and the significance of phonemes. Some texts discussed speech intelligibility, but primarily from a practical point of view without much attention to a theoretical background.

This lack of interest may be understandable, or even justifiable, in the more abstract studies on the attributes of tones and the ways in which they interfere with each other. These studies consisted, and mostly still do, of detection experiments in which the listener has to decide whether a stimulus is audible, or whether a difference between two stimuli can be perceived. For a rather long time, auditory research was characterized by *threshold* experiments. More recently, scaling techniques were added, particularly for the investigation of loudness and timbre. But this extension of the arsenal still did not explore the importance of listeners' previous experience with sound.

However, the experimenter crosses a borderline as soon as *recognition* begins to play a role. Whereas psychoacousticians in general can be content with detection and discrimination tasks, speech-perception scientists cannot. For them, to know *what* has been heard is far more interesting than to know *whether* anything was heard. From the beginning, speech researchers presented their subjects with natural or synthetic vowels, sometimes combined with initial and/or final consonants, in order to learn how phonemes were perceived. As vocal responses were rightly considered as less reliable, listeners were almost invariably asked to write down their responses. As earlier pointed out, this was, although for a quite different reason, at least as risky as trusting vocal responses. Recognition in this case was coupled with the listener's familiarity with spelling—it is remarkable that this bias has received so little attention in the literature. It is not difficult to find hundreds of papers in which this procedure has been adopted without a single word regarding the confounded nature of such responses. As shown in chapter 4, this disregard has led to misperceptions of the nature of the phoneme.

The neglect of cognitive factors has had consequences not only with respect to the conceptualization of phoneme perception, but also regarding how words and larger speech segments are perceived. By nature, the "auditory-only" approach is inclined to consider the spectrotemporal characteristics of the target stimulus as the sole, or at least most important, parameter determining a listener's response. Moreover, it is the most tempting approach in terms of simplicity. It is theoretically not attractive to admit that the perception of a target word is determined to a considerable degree by context.

This situation is illustrated by the early attempts to design automatic speech-recognizing systems. These efforts were directed by the expectation that careful analysis of the spectrotemporal characteristics of the speech signal was sufficient to obtain satisfactory results. In fact, the optimism for the possibilities of "reading" spectrograms was a first expression of the overestimation of the role of simple auditory processes in speech perception. The rather disappointing recognition scores that resulted compelled the engineers to turn their attention to the significant role of cognitive factors in speech recognition. The significance of context was the main topic of chapter 5. As the development of automatic speech recognizers had a substantial impact on the development of theories on speech perception, I consider them again later.

Bias 4. "Clean" Laboratory Conditions

As discussed in chapter 1, there are important reasons why conditions in the laboratory have to be rather different from those pertaining in everyday listening situations. It was also noted that this difference has its risks—distinctions between the two can be so great that the questions studied in the laboratory can become meager abstracts of reality, in which typical, even essential, qualities needed for everyday listening are overlooked.

The science of sound perception has not escaped this danger. Some important cases noted in the previous chapters have contributed to substantial delays in our understanding of the hearing process. Most can be explained as consequences of the theoretical underestimation of the role of masking. Masking patterns have been studied for a long time, but their significance in everyday listening has not received the attention it deserves.

One striking example is the search for the physical correlate of sound pitch. This point was discussed earlier as an example of the preference for using sinusoidal tones in hearing research. It is of interest to note that the main argument against the view that the pitch of a complex tone is based on its fundamental came from daily experience. Telephone engineers knew that the 300–3,400 Hz frequency band they employed in their systems did not include the fundamental of the speech sound—yet the transmitted speech signal had an unambiguous pitch. For a long time, this fact did not disturb the scientists. It was not until Licklider's (1954) demonstration at a meeting of the Acoustical Society of America, showing that a noise band completely masking the fundamental does not affect the perceived pitch, that the interest of the psychophysicists was aroused.[1] Looking back, it may surprise us that it took so long to dethrone the fundamental from its traditional position.

However, there are more striking examples of the disregard of daily conditions in laboratory experiments. We have all experienced the phenomenon that when two persons speak at the same time, each voice can sound virtually undisturbed by the presence of the other. It appears that, except in terms of intelligibility at unfavorable speech-to-noise ratios, the dynamically varying mutual

---

[1]As indicated in chapter 2, Licklider's demonstration actually resulted in a revival of Seebeck's periodicity theory before the pitch question found its final solution.

masking of spectral segments does not affect the continuity of the voices. This enigmatic phenomenon was discussed in chapters 3 and 5 as clear evidence of the active nature of the perceptual process. Keen observers such as Miller and Licklider (1950) were needed to focus our attention on this basic hearing quality, and other investigators had to make the same discovery before it received wider acceptance.

The third example can be seen as a consequence of the previous one. The significance of the continuity effect is not limited to the phenomenon as such. There is much more to say than that partially or fully masked sound segments are restored by the perceptual process as if they were actually present in the signal. Such restoration has theoretical implications regarding how speech is perceived. Even without any further experimental evidence, such as that reviewed in the previous chapter, we may conclude that our ability to understand speech where the audibility of individual phonemes is strongly affected by interfering sounds cannot be based simply on a linear process of identifying the successive phonemes. Just as the course of an old river bed can only be discovered from a certain height in an airplane, the course of the speech flow requires the "breadth" of several words before it can be recognized correctly. We have suggested the metaphor of a *listening window*, analogous to the visual window referred to in studies of reading.

SOUND PERCEPTION IS CATEGORICAL PERCEPTION

In chapter 4, I discussed an experiment by Liberman et al. (1957) in which listeners were asked to label 14 synthetic speechlike sounds representing small equal steps along the range of voiced consonants /b/–/d/–/g/, each followed by the vowel /e/. Most listeners tended to divide the continuum into three sharply defined phoneme categories. Pairs of stimuli differing by the same number of steps were much better discriminated at the phoneme boundaries than in the middle of a phoneme category. The authors interpreted this unequal discrimination of equal steps as evidence that the listeners had not been able to use a psychophysical criterion in this task but had instead based their decisions on the phoneme category. The phenomenon became known as *categorical perception*.

From a psychophysical point of view, this was indeed a rather remarkable result. Students of this discipline are used to finding that equal acoustic differences are reflected in (about) equal perceptual differences.[2] The categorical

---

[2]Equal steps may be understood as equal along a linear or a logarithmic scale, but this makes no essential difference here.

perception experiments indicated, however, that listeners showed uneven sensitivities (i.e., different at boundaries than within phoneme categories), suggesting that acoustic stimuli representing speech sounds do not necessarily obey psychophysical rules. Ergo: *Speech is special.*

Instead of engaging with the huge mass of experimental studies and the arguments pro and con the rigidity and specificity of categorical perception, I prefer to approach it from the more general angle of perceptual organization. We have seen that the identification of phonemes is biased by the listener's familiarity with the written alphabet. Therefore we cannot exclude the possibility that, similarly, the discrimination of phonemelike sounds, too, is influenced by our language experience. Let us consider the general characteristics of the perceptual strategy involved.

The function of our senses is to communicate with the outside world. This communication can be effective only if we know the code in which information is expressed. Conscious and unconscious interpretation are both essential. Vision offers a good example. A person who has never been exposed to modern traffic would be completely lost in one of our cities. We city dwellers, however, know what we see. We are acquainted with the objects, the cars, the traffic light, the safe sidewalks, and so on. We may not know the make of a car, but we are familiar with how it looks and how it may move. We need all this information in order to walk reasonably safely, by extrapolating what the other people, cars, and objects around us will do. In short, we label the visual objects in our environment on the basis of previous experience. This labeling makes possible meaningful (and safe) interaction with them.

Labeling means that we have learned the specific characteristics of an object. The "depth" of this knowledge can be quite different. Where a layman sees a flower, a gardener will recognize it as a begonia, and a biologist will know that it belongs to the nightshade family. Whether the labeling is coarse or fine is not essential; what is important is that, ideally, the nature of the label corresponds to the person's need to know how to deal with the object. We have to make decisions on a minute-by-minute (sometimes even second-by-second) basis, and we can make them only if we have sufficiently unambiguous knowledge provided by visual perception.

By definition, labeling is classification, allocation of the object to a category as a single entry out of a multiple of categories. Therefore, all perception is essentially *categorical perception.* We cannot permit ourselves to be only vaguely informed about our environment. Even in cases where we are not sure, we have to react, and this can be done only by cutting Gordian knots, by allocating objects to what may be the wrong categories. This is the price we have to pay in order to stay alive. We have to decide whether a car may hit us or not, but we have no guarantee that we are right.

In more mathematical terms, now well known from their applications in computers, we may say that, perceptually, we are permanently engaged as analog-to-digital converters, translating the gently flowing picture of lines and colors on our retina as best as we can back into the discrete objects we believe to exist in the world around us. The more accurate this translation is, the more appropriately we are able to react.

Direct evidence of this role of translation, to be considered as *interpretation*, in hearing is the continuity effect discussed in chapter 3. A tone interrupted periodically by bursts of noise is still heard as a continuous tone. The auditory system makes its own decisions in terms of probability about sounds being received, and for the most part it is right. It "tells" us that the same tone is sounding continuously, although there is a (theoretical) chance that what was actually presented was a series of isolated tone bursts. As mentioned in chapter 3, our expectations can change what we hear. Again, categorical perception, in the general sense of the term, can be seen as a basic quality of the perceptual system.

This strategy is not only an intrinsic property of perception, irrespective of our will or past experience, but, as has become convincingly clear for speech, is also a reinforced and acquired property. The auditory perceptual process is constantly restoring mutilated speech fragments on the basis of earlier experiences as well as the expectations of the listener. Absent phonemes are "automatically" replaced with the most probable candidates deduced from longer speech segments. There is no compelling acoustical reason to hear *legi▮lature* as *legislature* (Warren's demonstration), but we do. The listener wants to know what the speaker has said, and the hearing process meets this desire by combining all pieces of information available for an acceptable solution. The result can be wrong, but the perception process takes the risk.

This perceptual behavior implies that both vision and audition are biased senses. Rather than looking and hearing with an open mind, we are always interpreting, unconsciously as well as consciously, what we see and hear. It means that we may attach much more weight to one feature than to another. We believe that a visual object remains the same, whether close by or at a large distance—size constancy is a basic property of the system. We appear to know quite well which differences in vowel sounds are significant and which are not. We may hesitate in an abstract laboratory experiment, but we do not in conversational speech. Again, this is categorical perception in the fullest sense of the term.

Only now does it make sense to return to the first paragraph of this section, where this term was used to explain a discrepancy between labeling and discriminating phonemelike sounds. Actually, two entirely different paradigms were involved. As explained, labeling is a *natural* act, and the labeling of phonemelike sounds can be seen as perfectly in agreement with what the hearing system is expected to do. However, this does not hold for the discrimination of these sounds. Measuring just-noticeable differences is a highly sophisticated act, dear to laboratory testing but seldom practiced elsewhere. This is quite evident in the reports of discrimination experiments, where the reader is informed how many hours of training were required for listeners to perform at asymptotic response levels.

Should we expect that test subjects will be able to discriminate two phonemelike sounds as reliably as any other pair of nonsense sounds? To answer this question, it is revealing to study the comments made by Liberman and his colleagues themselves. In the first place, as noted by Lane (1965), it was apparently typical for these authors to reject about half the recruited subjects as not meeting criteria for acceptance into the studies. Even in those tested, individual differences were found. The 1957 study noted:

> Clearly, the data obtained with this S[ubject] are not all so neat and striking as the particular examples chosen, and some of the other Ss were more variable, especially in their responses to the discrimination task.... It is, nevertheless, reasonably apparent from an inspection of the data of all Ss that the discriminations tend to be relatively more acute in the vicinity of phoneme boundaries than in the middle of phoneme categories. (p. 362)

In the second place, it is important to remember that these results were obtained with stop consonants, the phonemes that appear to be most susceptible to the effect. The theoretical value of categorical perception posited as a unique property of speech loses its cogency in the light of the fact that it could not be demonstrated for vowels or other consonants (Fry, Abramson, Eimas, & Liberman, 1962).

Moreover, other investigators who tried to repeat the stop-consonant experiments came to divergent conclusions. Pisoni and Lazarus (1974) described an experiment by Cross and Lane, who found that discrimination functions for subjects who were not told they were listening to (synthetic) speech stimuli did not show the categorical effect. From these and their own results, Pisoni and Lazarus concluded that the categorical perception effect depends on the testing procedure used. Samuel (1977), using both untrained and trained listeners, observed that training could substantially improve the discrimination of stop-consonant-like stimuli labeled as the same phoneme. His experiments confirmed that there are large interindividual differences in overall level of performance, as implicitly admitted earlier by Liberman et al. (1957).

These observations make it reasonable to conclude that the phenomenon traditionally denoted as categorical perception is the result of expectation, experience and training. It is quite conceivable that the natural inclination to perceive acoustically slightly different speech sounds as the same phoneme is so strong that it overrules the general auditory capacity to discriminate them as different sounds. There is evidence supporting this view.

In the first place, it appears that the phenomenon is not restricted to speech sounds. Both Siegel and Siegel (1977) and Burns and Ward (1978) found that musicians were very poor in differentiating tonal intervals within the same musical category. Second, trained monkeys and birds respond to phonemelike sounds in ways that are similar to human test subjects (reviewed by Kuhl, 1987a). Given these observations, the categorical-perception effect as evidence for a special speech perception code loses much of its power. The experiments strongly suggest that, indeed, the seeming discrepancy between labeling and discriminating phonemelike sounds is an artifact of the subjects' long experience listening to spoken language.

SOUND PERCEPTION AS A FORM
OF OBJECT PERCEPTION

In the previous section we saw that our perception is continuously "reconstructing" the discrete objects of the outside world on the basis of the more or less continuous information received via our senses. The endless stream of sound is structured into patterns to tell us as reliably as possible what is going on around us, which sounds belong together and which are produced by different sources. Seemingly unconnected fragments are linked together to form patterns to which meanings can be attached. Sound perception was characterized in the previous chapters as a holistic rather than an elementalistic process. Every chapter provided ample evidence for it: the perception of pitch and timbre in chapter 2, the continuity effect and the segregation of sound streams in chapter 3, the positive role of coarticulation in chapter 4, and the significance of context in chapter 5. Although such terms have not been used here before, the reader may have concluded from our examples that sound perception, like visual perception, is controlled by the well-known gestalt principles of proximity, similarity, continuity, and common fate.

It may seem tempting to accept this conclusion without further comment. We will see, however, that these respectable century-old principles are not as solid as traditionally believed. Surprisingly, as research of the last decades has shown, they suffer from a disease similar to that described for the phoneme concept. Whereas ideas regarding phoneme perception were biased by knowledge of the written alphabet, gestalt principles may represent not only innate perceptual features but also qualities acquired by experience.

One means of avoiding a possible experience bias is to test infants. An interesting visual experiment with 4-month-old infants was done by Kellman and Spelke (1983). The question was related to the principle of continuity: Adults see the lower and upper lines in Fig. 6.1 as parts of single straight lines interrupted by the box—is this also true for infants? Using "looking time" as a dependent variable, the authors concluded that infants do not see in the same way as adults do. For example, they seem to see the two parts of a rod with its center part covered by a block (the condition of Fig. 6.1) not as a single rod, but as two rods. However, when lateral movements of the rod were introduced, a *single* rod seemed to be perceived. Apparently common motion was a necessary condition to see continuity.[3]

As might be expected, it was a challenge to repeat such tests with even younger infants. Slater et al. (1990) succeeded in training newborns sufficiently to show that for them the two visible parts of the rod, even when moving, did *not* represent a single object. These authors concluded that, unlike 4-month-old infants, "newborns appear to perceive only that which is immediately visible, and they seem to be unable to make perceptual inferences from visual input" (p. 33).

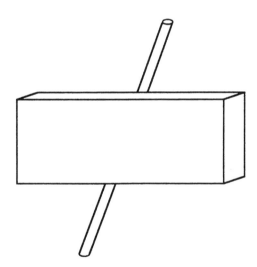

FIG. 6.1.   Display of a rod behind a block, used by Kellman and Spelke (1983) in their experiments with infants.

---

[3]It would be of interest to know the extent to which young children exhibit the perceptual effect illustrated in Figs. 6.1 and 6.2 in their own drawings.

Spelke, Breinlinger, Macomber, and Jacobson (1992) used these and additional observations to explore "the origins of knowledge." The first paragraph of their general discussion is of particular interest:

> The present experiments support the active representations thesis: They provide evidence that capacities to represent and reason about the physical world develop at an early age, in parallel with capacities to perceive and act. At 3 and 4 months of age, infants are not able to talk about objects, produce and understand object-directed gestures, locomote around objects, reach for and manipulate objects, or even see objects with high resolution. Nevertheless, such infants can represent an object that has left their view and make inferences about its occluded motion. In particular, infants represent objects and reason about object motions in accord with two constraints on the behavior of material bodies: continuity and solidity. (pp. 626–627)

I believe that these studies have direct relevance for speech perception. In the first place, they throw new light on the gestalt principles, usually considered as basic, inborn qualities of perception. The experiments indicate that these qualities are not as immediate and self-evident as has been thought. These findings strongly suggest that at least some gestalt qualities are learned rather than innate.

Second, the experiments also show that these principles, as learned qualities, have their origin in the perception of *three-dimensional objects* of the outer world rather than the two-dimensional pictures projected on our retina. Perceiving two separate line segments as parts of a continuous line (Fig. 6.1) represents a two-dimensional projection of a solid box in front of a stick. We are so familiar with drawings and pictures that it is easy for them to take on the status of a new reality on their own, whereas they are actually no more than artifactual products with which we try to record an image of the "real" three-dimensional visual world. Figures 6.2 and 6.3 illustrate this. We don't see the first figure as just a set of lines but as a collection of flat pieces of paper partly covering each other. The lines in the second figure clearly group themselves as three-dimensional objects. We may say that our perception is predisposed to structure any image on the retina in terms of *objects*. The question of the extent to which this particular feature of visual perception is innate or learned is not important here. Because the outer world consists of objects, the predisposition to see sets of visual elements as representations of objects is the most efficient and effective way of handling and interpreting visual stimuli.

The Spelke et al. conclusion suggests that our perceptual systems come predisposed to function in a world of objects, and that visual information alone controls the infant's perception even before the child has had the opportunity to verify the existence of three-dimensional objects by other means. This is yet

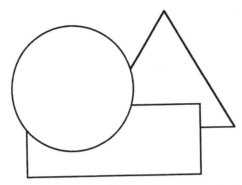

FIG. 6.2.   Drawing seen as three pieces of paper partly covering each other.

another example of the active nature of our perception, designed and prepared for its task in life.

We may expect that what holds for visual perception also holds for hearing. We demonstrated in chapter 4 that young infants are remarkably able to discriminate speech sounds and to distinguish between their essential and nonessential properties. Similarly as in vision, the infant has to learn to live in a world of sounds that must be distinguished on the basis of their specific characteristics. Although there is at the moment no clear evidence that young infants hear continuous tones straight through masking bursts of noise, we do know that as soon as they begin to grasp the meaning of speech they seem to be well prepared for this task and are

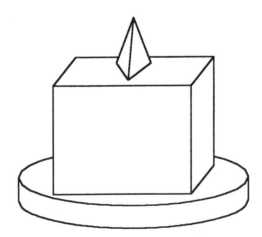

FIG. 6.3.   Drawing seen as three-dimensional objects on top of each other.

able to separate relevant from irrelevant sounds. For young children, as for us, sounds in the environment carry information about "auditory objects."

Auditory perception is much more than the addition of elementary sensations. As shown in chapter 3, it too obeys gestalt principles. Just as the eye organizes visual stimuli into a representation, a "picture" of the visual objects in the outside world, the ear reconstructs from the mixed incoming fragments a "picture" of the various sounds comprising the incoming mixture—auditory objects to be learned and recognized.

THE PROMINENCE AS WELL AS THE FLEXIBILITY OF TIMBRE

Timbre, pitch, and loudness were discussed in chapter 2 as the three main attributes of sounds. All three are predominantly auditory, depending only in a minor way on cognition. They can be studied quite successfully in the laboratory as robust attributes of sounds, and their perception seems to be essentially independent of a listener's age, social background, and experience.

This robustness should not mislead us into believing these features are equally vulnerable or invulnerable to the acoustic conditions of everyday life. As shown in the previous chapters, cognitive factors are certainly very important in sound perception. Therefore, it makes sense to ask whether, and to what extent, the three basic attributes of sound are affected by the distortions and disturbances that are unavoidable in real life.

Without doubt, pitch is the most invariable attribute of tones. Apart from the Doppler effect observed for moving sound sources, the number of source vibrations per second is not affected by the acoustic transmission path to the listener. Laboratory tests have shown that the pitch of a sinusoidal tone may depend slightly on its amplitude, but the effect is of no consequence in everyday hearing. Even electronically, sound frequency is quite resistant to the common types of linear and nonlinear distortions.

A quite different behavior is seen for loudness. Differences in distance to a sound source correspond to differences in loudness. We are so adapted to this variability that we usually consider loudness as a characteristic of the source (we "adjust for distance") rather than of the sound itself. Nevertheless, loudness becomes important when we are comparing the relative loudnesses of simultaneous sounds. As we have seen, the perceptibility of a sound is determined by its signal-to-noise ratio, and as long as this ratio remains constant, audibility remains constant.

Timbre is the attribute of sounds that is most vulnerable to interference. It is considered here in the broadest sense of the term, to include all spectral and temporal characteristics of sound other than pitch and loudness. It is almost impossible to transmit a sound without changing its spectrotemporal properties, and thus its timbre. The acoustics of the environment and the specifications of electronic transmission systems can modify the signal substantially. Reverberation can result in spectral uncertainties with a standard deviation of up to 5.7 dB for every tonal component (Plomp & Steeneken, 1973), and can also smooth rapid temporal variations of the signal. Whereas pitch remains unaffected and loudness can be restored, most timbre distortions are irreversible.

At the same time, timbre can be considered to be the primary carrier of auditory information, particularly for listening to speech. The voices of men, women, and children differ considerably in their pitch ranges, but this has no effect on intelligibility. Vowels are mainly determined by their spectral characteristics and consonants by their temporal characteristics.

The paradox posed by these two characteristics of timbre—at once the most vulnerable and the most informative attribute of sounds—may appear to be a very serious problem. If we restrict ourselves to the auditory aspects, it would imply that successful speech perception requires that timbre be faithfully preserved. However, this is not the case. As we have seen, variations in pronunciation are so large that roughly only half of the phonemes in fluent speech are individually identifiable. Yet the speech signal is so redundant that it can be distorted quite substantially, spectrally as well as temporally, before becoming unintelligible. The uncertainty of the speech signal in a psychophysical sense is more than compensated for by the large role played by cognition.

This solution of the perceptual problem has an interesting aspect. It means that, whereas we can trust pitch and (restored) loudness as faithfully representing features of the sound source, this does not hold for timbre. We hear immediately that a telephone-transmitted voice lacks its high-frequency components and that a voice in a reverberating room has been stripped of its fast transients, but these deviations from strictly accurate representation do not seem to bother the listener very much. This flexibility of the listener means that timbre, or at least its underlying spectrotemporal correlates, is an unreliable characteristic of speech sounds as such.

It might seem that this point is so obvious that there is no need to elaborate on it. However, it appears that the consequences of this conclusion have been overlooked for a long time and may be still difficult for some workers in the field to accept. This is particularly true regarding efforts to design machines for automatic speech recognition.

Attempts to design such machines have invariably used spectral differences between speech sounds as the salient cues. The introduction of computers made it possible to quantify these differences at such a rate that the recognition of spoken words in real time became possible. I illustrate this development with the approach I know best.

We saw in chapter 2 that timbre dissimilarities between vowel sounds are highly correlated with their spectral differences analyzed in terms of principal components. Based on this finding, Klein, Plomp, and Pols (1970) used 18 filter bands, each $^1/_3$ octave wide, to analyze 12 Dutch vowels in the words h(*vowel*)t pronounced by 50 male speakers. A principal-components analysis revealed that 75.4% of the variance could be explained by four components. Subsequently, the authors developed an algorithm for automatic recognition of the 600 vowel sounds on the basis of the spectra measured. In this way, it was possible to learn how many components are required for reliable identification (see Fig. 6.4). Three components appeared to be sufficient to obtain more than 97% correct identifications, considered to be a very encouraging result.

The next step was taken by Pols (1971), who extended the technique to 20 words. The idea was that if a vowel can be geometrically represented by a *point*, a word can be represented by a *trace* in a multidimensional space, with the principal components as the axes. The words were spectrally analyzed in successive samples of 15 msec, short enough to follow faithfully the dynamic variations of the sound. Every word has its own trace, and the best agreement of a new trace with the "standard" traces or templates for the 20 words can be used as an estimate of the corresponding word pronounced. Pols found that more than 95% of the 20 words, each newly pronounced by 20 speakers, were correctly recognized.

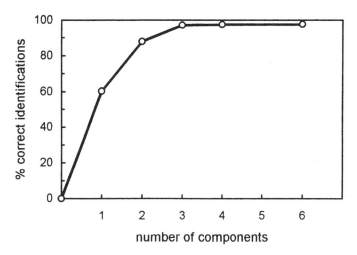

FIG. 6.4. Identification score of 12 Dutch vowels, each pronounced by 50 male speakers, obtained with a principle-components analysis of their spectra, plotted as a function of the number of components taken into account (redrawn from Klein, Plomp, & Pols, 1970).

These scores, again, may seem encouraging, but there are many questions yet to be asked. One of them concerns which measure should be used to express the spectral intensities. Bladon and Lindblom (1981) preferred loudness rather than the logarithmic (dB) measure used in the experiments referred to above. Zahorian and Rothenberg (1981), applying the principal-components procedure to continuous speech, actually compared different measures. They observed that their resynthesized speech sounded best with a logarithmic measure, confirming the earlier choice.

Although these evaluations may seem reassuring, there are other, much more serious problems with respect to the template approach. At least the following five must be addressed:

1. *Coarticulation*. The transients between the vowels and "ideal" target consonants manifest themselves as different traces in the multidimensional space (Schouten & Pols, 1979).

2. *Temporal variations*. There is great inter- as well as intraindividual freedom in the temporal structure of the same word. The word to be recognized has to be subjected to so-called *dynamic time warping* in order to align the time axis with the templates. As the temporal characteristics of consonants are at least as important as their spectral characteristics, this information should not be lost in the warping procedure.

3. *Word boundaries*. As history has shown, the step from automatic recognition of isolated words to words in sentences is an almost insurmountable barrier. The successive sound samples do not provide the machine with information as to where one word ends and the next begins.

4. *Pronunciation variability*. As would be expected from our discussions in chapter 5, the differences in pronunciation present in spoken language are too large to be matched against general phoneme-based templates.

5. *Distortions and disturbances*. Lacking very sophisticated measures, templates are unable to cope with the substantial maltreatments to which the speech signal is frequently subjected, including interference from other sounds, which may mask fragments of the signal.

Confronted with these problems, we have to admit that automatic speech recognition on the basis of templates is a very precarious adventure. In discussing its possibilities, Klatt (1982) rightly considered that spectral tilt, high-pass and low-pass filtering, and so on were incompatible with the spectral distance metric proposed above. As he concluded, this metric "that works reasonably well in predicting psychophysical distance judgements does not work at all well in predicting phonetic distance" (p. 1281). But is it reasonable to expect, as Klatt seemed to do, that there are other metrics that can meet the objections described?

Actually, the discrepancy between spectral distances and phonetic distances should not worry us as a unique phenomenon. We should be aware that the insufficiency of the psychophysical parameters of a stimulus for explaining its identification or recognition is a general, one might even say *essential*, characteristic of perception. Perhaps the most striking example is the discrepancy that we tolerate contrasting a photograph and a drawing of the same person or object. Psychophysically, for example, in terms of the brightness distribution in two dimensions, the two representations are quite different, but in terms of recognition, they are very similar.

It seems to me that we have here a classic example of our "natural" inclination (I include myself as an originally rather optimistic adherent of the template approach) to undervalue the dangers of one-sidedness discussed in the first section of this chapter. As explained, these dangers include the temptations to overlook the need for a macroscopic approach, the cognitive aspects of perception, and the importance of "dirty" everyday conditions. Overlooking the macroscopic approach consisted of a too strong emphasis on the power of the phoneme, the underestimation of cognitive aspects was represented by an unjustified belief that speech recognition can be satisfactorily dealt with in terms of audition alone, and everyday conditions were ignored when scientists sought to exclude distortions and competing sounds. All three points are pertinent with respect to the template concept.

As has been demonstrated extensively in chapter 5, context is so essential for human speech recognition that we should not suppose an automatic system can do without it. The development of mechanical recognizers has been possible only by providing the systems with (a) a large vocabulary, nowadays even up to 300,000 items, and (b) statistical probability measures regarding the occurrence of word combinations. Nevertheless, even when optimized for individual voices, these devices are only moderately reliable for open speech sets, demonstrating that they are still primitive compared with the human listener armed with knowledge of language and expectations of what might be said, both exceeding by far the capabilities of any statistical criterion. The gap between automatic recognition systems and an adult human listener seems to be unbridgeable when we consider the differences in their ability to cope with speech mutilations or disturbing sounds, for example, in the case of a single competing speaker.

THEORETICAL SPECULATIONS

Traditionally, books on the psychophysics of hearing contain a chapter on the anatomy and physiology of the auditory system. As long as attention was limited primarily to the perception of sinusoidal sounds, knowledge about how the peripheral ear resolves sounds into such components, how sinusoids initiate action potentials, and how these potentials are transmitted through the auditory nerve to higher centers could be considered as presenting sufficient insight into how the auditory system works.

Nowadays, the poverty of this approach is becoming more and more obvious. As we have seen, the phenomena we have to explain are much more complex than the perception of simple tones. They begin with pitch and timbre and culminate in the continuity effect and the segregation of sound streams, now recognized as basic properties of auditory perception. We have no clear concepts of how these processes are perceptually achieved, let alone which physiological mechanisms are involved. Handel (1989) ended his chapter on auditory physiology, the last in his book on hearing, with the confession:

> When I first imagined writing this book, I thought there would be elegant connections between perceptual variables and physiological cells. I thought that it would be possible to discover acoustic features (which might be quite complex) for events and to discover physiological analyzers that signal these features. But as I began to appreciate the inherent context dependency of perceiving, it dawned on me that a fundamentally different model of cortical functioning was necessary. Because of the complexity of the acoustic signal, a relatively static organization into centers would be inadequate and inappropriate. A flexible organizational system, able to capitalize on the regularities in the acoustic signal caused by the constraints on production, would be necessary. Giving up the concept of a hierarchical organization leaves the problem of how the multiple representations yield a coherent percept. That is still a mystery. (pp. 544–545)

I agree with this conclusion.

The notion that hearing is a highly complex process has been underlined by the difficulties of designing speech-recognizing systems. As discussed in the preceding section, such efforts started with rather naive ideas that speech perception could be fully explained in terms of the ear's powers of frequency resolution as visualized in the spectrogram. This was a misjudgment of the real psychophysical power of the auditory system as well as the significant role played by cognitive factors in hearing.

With respect to the first misjudgment, it must be realized that the spectrogram does not approach a fair representation of the psychophysics of the ear. It represents no more than the frequency resolution of the peripheral ear as a first stage of the auditory process, whereas the actual percepts are characterized by distinct qualities of pitch and timbre, both products of higher level processing. Also, a one-sided emphasis on the spectral aspects of sound underestimates temporal aspects that are at least as important. Moreover, the spectrogram does not take account of the perceptual system's ability to segregate sounds, or the continuity effect with its power to restore masked speech segments. There is a fundamental difference between the perception of simultaneous voices in a discussion or concert, and the spectrogram as the visual representation of recorded sound. Actually, the spectrogram is a very poor picture of the ear's information-processing power. In this light, it is not surprising that tactile and other alternative presentations of the speech signal to the deaf, based on only those sound features portrayed in the spectrogram, have never led to satisfying results.

The second misjudgment is at least as fatal as the first. The prevailing interest in the perception of isolated speech elements as opposed to fluent speech had led to a general underestimation of cognition in hearing. Linguists contributed to the recovery of some balance in this regard, but the disappointing results of the early speech-recognizing systems may have been the major driving force toward acknowledging the importance of cognition. The systems available now are provided with huge vocabularies as well as linguistic and statistic rules in order to take full account of context.

This technical background of the interest in the cognitive role in speech perception has contributed considerably to our present insights regarding how sounds are perceived. It has demonstrated convincingly that no model of speech perception can ignore the role of context (Moore, 1981), and thus has led to significant improvements in what were originally rather primitive concepts.

The more recent models can be roughly divided in two groups on the basis of their leitmotiv. Some models betray the more technical background, reflecting the state of the art of automatic speech recognizers; others are derived from a more computational background, inspired by the philosophies of parallel processing and artificial intelligence. Both schools give ample attention to phonemes, albeit in different ways. The first approach tries to trace the phonemes more directly on the bases of their features. The best known example is Klatt's (1989) LAFS model, according to which words in long-term memory must "somehow" be represented in terms of spectral templates. The second approach conceptualizes networks of brain cells that have learned to distinguish auditory inputs. For example, in the TRACE model, developed by McClelland and Elman (1986), information processing takes place via excitatory and inhibitory interactions of a large number of simple processing units, each working continuously to update its own activation on the basis of the activations of other units to which it is connected (for recent reviews see Lively, Pisoni, & Goldinger, 1994; Massaro, 1994). More recently, Norris (1994) proposed his shortlist model as an improvement of TRACE. All three models have in common that they are positioned much nearer to the left end of the elementalistic–holistic scale than seems to be justified by the experimental evidence presented in the previous chapters. For instance, the shortlist model is, as its author says, "entirely bottom-up," which appears to mean that the role of the context is limited to the contribution of the direct neighbors of a word as cues to its boundaries.

The latter example shows that the propensity to approach the *macroscopic* phenomenon of the perception of fluent speech with *microscopic* concepts is almost irresistible. This is also apparent in the experimental procedures employed. Cutler and Norris (1988) introduced "word spotting" as a useful laboratory task in studying the segmentation process of connected speech. They presented their subjects with lists of bisyllabic nonwords, only some of which contained a meaningful word as the first syllable (e.g., *bozzem* and *mintesh*, respectively). The listeners' task was to press a response key whenever they heard a nonsense word beginning with a real word. It is not clear what this single-word task has to do with recognizing the successive real words in fluent speech. In the latter case, the listener makes ample use of the context corresponding with a moving time "window" of more than 1 sec, as we have seen in the previous chapter. Moreover, the constraint to react as soon as possible presupposes a quite different listening strategy than used in normal hearing. We will never discover the role of semantics in listening as long as we do not include this factor, and other possibly relevant factors, in our experimental approach.

The continuing predilection of speech scientists to seek to explain the intelligibility of connected speech as a linear process of word recognition is remarkable. It may look attractive as a valid solution following the failures of earlier explanations of speech perception based on phoneme identification (chap. 4), but it is still rather unsatisfactory. If the perception and production of speech are closely connected processes, we may expect that listening reflects speaking in its fullest extent. We do not speak by thinking up words one by one, or even in combinations of two, but by considering much longer phrases in order to generate grammatically correct sentences, with proper intonation and stress, where earlier words are chosen to match later words. We can be sure that these mutual relations controlling the production of speech play a similar role in its perception. Context dominates both processes.

We must conclude that the attempts to date to mold the experimental evidence into a theoretical framework are not very convincing. There are no compelling reasons why our brains might function similarly to a technical tool working at a much lower level of sophistication. It has become more and more clear that, in contrast to speech-recognizing systems, brains are not provided with an ensemble of centers, each dedicated to a special aspect of perception.

There are many ways in which machines have been made to mimic human performance, such as moving and writing, but the performance goals are reached by quite different means in mechanical as opposed to biological systems. It is shocking to see how crudely robots perform even in accomplishing what are for us very simple tasks such as grasping an object.

In this respect, the network approach mentioned may seem more promising. However, at the moment these networks are entirely hypothetical. We need much more information regarding the brain activities involved in perception if we are to improve and correct network models. The study of a living neural network means that activity at a large number of locations has to be recorded at the same time as ongoing perception, and this raises a host of methodological problems that have yet to be solved. In the meantime, we may have to accept that perception is a "black box," with reasonably well-known inputs and outputs but an unknown interior.

The problem of a black box is that we cannot enter it to discover how the perceptual process is structured. Model makers can do no better than try to conclude from the overall performance how the inside is organized. The result is invariably a set of interconnected boxes, with each box conceptualized to represent a specific subcomponent of the overall process. Scientifically, this is unsatisfactory. Such a model is too vague to allow unequivocal predictions, and it is therefore impossible to verify its reality. As Uttal (1988) argued for visual form perception, it is doubtful whether science will ever be able to unravel the secrets of the black box of the perception of sounds.

A major difficulty is that here again, as we have seen often before, theoretical speculations are invariably too one-sidedly based on "clean" laboratory conditions. Certainly exploring the role of context is not an easy task, and it is even more difficult to study what makes speech perception so resistant to mutilation and masking. It is understandable that model makers neglect these complications, but it can also be asked whether a model of perception designed without these complications in mind can ever be adequate. Coping successfully with disturbances appears to be such a basic achievement of the hearing system that any viable theory must take full account of it right from the beginning.

References

Ash, M. G. (1995). *Gestalt psychology in German culture, 1890–1967.* Cambridge, UK: Cambridge University Press.

Baer, T., & Moore, B. C. J. (1993). Effects of spectral smearing on the intelligibility of sentences in noise. *Journal of the Acoustical Society of America, 94,* 1229–1241.

Bagley, W. C. (1900–1901). The apperception of the spoken sentence: A study in the psychology of language. *American Journal of Psychology, 12,* 80–130.

Bard, E. G., Shillcock, R. C., & Altmann, G. T. M. (1988). The recognition of words after their acoustic offsets in spontaneous speech: Effects of subsequent context. *Perception & Psychophysics, 44,* 395–408.

Bashford, J. A., Riener, K. R., & Warren, R. M. (1992). Increasing the intelligibility of speech through multiple phonemic restorations. *Perception & Psychophysics, 51,* 211–217.

Bashford, J. A., & Warren, R. M. (1987). Multiple phonemic restorations follow the rules for auditory induction. *Perception & Psychophysics, 42,* 114–121.

Bates, E., & Goodman, J. C. (1997). On the inseparability of grammar and the lexicon: Evidence from acquisition, Aphasia and real-time processing. *Language and Cognitive Processes, 12,* 507–584.

Beauvois, M. W., & Meddis, R. (1997). Time decay of auditory stream biasing. *Perception & Psychophysics, 59,* 81–86.

Benedict, H. (1979). Early lexical development: Comprehension and production. *Journal of Child Language, 6,* 183–200.

Besner, D. (1987). On the relationship between orthographies and phonologies in visual word recognition. In A. Allport, D. MacKay, W. Prinz, & E. Scheerer (Eds.), *Language perception and production* (pp. 211–226). London: Academic Press.

Best, C. T., Morrongiello, B., & Robson, R. (1981). Perceptual equivalence of acoustic cues in speech and nonspeech perception. *Perception & Psychophysics, 29,* 191–211.

Bladon, R. A. W., & Lindblom, B. (1981). Modeling the judgment of vowel quality differences. *Journal of the Acoustical Society of America, 69,* 1414–1422.

Blauert, J. (1983). *Spatial hearing—The psychophysics of human sound localization.* Cambridge, MA: MIT Press.

Bloom, L. (1993). *The transition from infancy to language—Acquiring the power of expression.* Cambridge, UK: Cambridge University Press.

Blumstein, S. E., & Stevens, K. N. (1979). Acoustic invariance in speech production: Evidence from measurements of the spectral characteristics of stop consonants. *Journal of the Acoustical Society of America, 66,* 1001–1016.

Blumstein, S. E., & Stevens, K. N. (1980). Perceptual invariance and onset spectra for stop consonants in different vowel environments. *Journal of the Acoustical Society of America, 67,* 648–662.

Breeuwer, M., & Plomp, R. (1986). Speech reading supplemented with auditorily presented speech parameters. *Journal of the Acoustical Society of America, 79,* 481–499.

Bregman, A. S. (1990). *Auditory scene analysis—The perceptual organization of sound.* Cambridge, MA: MIT Press.

Bregman, A. S., & Dannenbring, G. L. (1973). The effect of continuity on auditory stream segregation. *Perception & Psychophysics, 13,* 308–312.

Bronkhorst, A. W., & Plomp, R. (1988). The effect of head-induced interaural time and level differences on speech intelligibility in noise. *Journal of the Acoustical Society of America, 83,* 1508–1516.

Bronkhorst, A. W., & Plomp, R. (1992). Effect of multiple speechlike maskers on binaural speech recognition in normal and impaired hearing. *Journal of the Acoustical Society of America, 92,* 3132–3139.

Bruce, D.J. (1964). The analysis of word sounds by young children. *British Journal of Educational Psychology, 34,* 158–170.

Burns, E. M., & Ward, W. D. (1978). Categorical perception—phenomenon or epiphenomenon: Evidence from experiments in the perception of melodic musical intervals. *Journal of the Acoustical Society of America, 63,* 456–468.

Byrne, B., & Fielding-Barnsley, R. (1989). Phonemic awareness and letter knowledge in the child's acquisition of the alphabetic principle. *Journal of Educational Psychology, 81,* 313–321.

Carey, S. (1978). The child as a word reader. In M. Halle, J. Bresnan, & G. Miller (Eds.), *Linguistic theory and psychological reality* (pp. 264–293). Cambridge, MA: MIT Press.

Cattell, J. M. (1885). Ueber die Zeit der Erkennung und Benennung von Schriftzeichen, Bildern und Farben. *Philosophische Studien, 2,* 635–650. English translation in Poffenberger (1947).

Chall, J. S. (1967). *Learning to read: The great debate.* New York: McGraw-Hill.

Cherry, C., & Wiley, R. (1967). Speech communication in very noisy environments. *Nature, 214,* 1164.

Ciocca, V., & Bregman, A. S. (1987). Perceived continuity of gliding and steady-state tones through interrupting noise. *Perception & Psychophysics, 42,* 476–484.

Clark, E. V. (1995). Language Acquisition: The lexicon and syntax. In J. L. Miller & P. D. Eimas (Eds.), *Handbook of perception and cognition: Speech, language, and communication* (2nd ed., pp. 303–337). San Diego, CA: Academic Press.

Cohen, G. (1989). *Memory in the real world.* Hillsdale, NJ: Lawrence Erlbaum Associates.

Cole, R. A., & Jakimik, J. (1978). Understanding speech: How words are heard. In G. Underwood (Ed.), *Strategies of information processing* (pp. 67–116). London: Academic Press.

Cole, R. A., & Rudnicky, A. I. (1983). What's new in speech perception? The research and ideas of William Chandler Bagley, 1874–1946. *Psychological Review, 90,* 94–101.

Cole, R. A., Rudnicky, A. I., Zue, V. W., & Reddy, D. R. (1980). Speech as patterns on paper. In R. A. Cole (Ed.), *Perception and production of fluent speech* (pp. 3–50). Hillsdale, NJ: Lawrence Erlbaum Associates.

Cole, R. A., & Scott, B. (1973). Perception of temporal order in speech: The role of vowel transitions. *Canadian Journal of Psychology, 27,* 441–449.

Coulmas, F. (1989). *The writing systems of the world.* Oxford, UK: Blackwell.

Crystal, T. H., & House, A. S. (1988a). The duration of American-English vowels: An overview. *Journal of Phonetics, 16,* 263–284.

Crystal, T. H., & House, A. S. (1988b). The duration of American-English stop consonants: An overview. *Journal of Phonetics, 16,* 285–294.

Crystal, T. H., & House, A. S. (1990). Articulation rate and the duration of syllables and stress groups in connected speech. *Journal of the Acoustical Society of America, 88,* 101–112.

Cutler, A. (1995). Spoken word recognition and production. In J. L. Miller and P. D. Eimas (Eds.), *Handbook of perception and cognition: Speech, language, and communication* (2nd ed., pp. 97–136). San Diego, CA: Academic Press.

Cutler, A., & Norris, D. (1988). The role of strong syllables in segmentation for lexical access. *Journal of Experimental Psychology: Human Perception and Performance, 14,* 113–121.

Dannenbring, G. L. (1976). Perceived auditory continuity with alternately rising and falling frequency transitions. *Canadian Journal of Psychology, 30,* 99–114.

Darwin, C. J. (1984). Perceiving vowels in the presence of another sound: Constraints on formant perception. *Journal of the Acoustical Society of America, 76,* 1636–1647.

de Boer, E. (1956). *On the "residue" in hearing.* Doctoral thesis, University of Amsterdam.

de Boysson-Bardies, B., Hallé, P., Sagart, L., & Durand, C. (1989). A cross-linguistic investigation of vowel formants in babbling. *Journal of Child Language, 16,* 1–17.

de Waard, C. (1946). *Correspondance de P. Marin Mersenne, religieux minime,* Vol. 3. Paris, Presses Universitaires de France.

Diehl, R. L., Kluender, K. R., Foss, D. J., Parker, E. M., & Gernsbacher, M. A. (1987). Vowels as islands of reliability. *Journal of Memory and Language, 26,* 564–573.

Dorman, M. F., Cutting, J. E., & Raphael, L. J. (1975). Perception of temporal order in vowel sequences with and without formant transitions. *Journal of Experimental Psychology: Human Perception and Performance, 104,* 121–129.

Dorman, M. F., Loizou, P. C., & Rainey, D. (1997). Speech intelligibility as a function of the number of channels of stimulation for signal processors using sine-wave and noise-band outputs. *Journal of the Acoustical Society of America, 102,* 2403–2411.

Downing, J. (1973). Linguistic environments, II. In J. Downing (Ed.), *Comparative reading—Cross-national studies of behavior and processes in reading and writing* (pp. 217–243). New York: Macmillan.

Downing, J., & Leong, C. K. (1982). *Psychology of reading.* New York: Macmillan.

Driver, G. R. (1948). *Semitic writing—From pictographs to alphabet.* London: Oxford University Press.

Drullman, R., Festen, J. M., & Plomp, R. (1994). Effect of temporal envelope smearing on speech reception. *Journal of the Acoustical Society of America, 95,* 1053–1064.

Duquesnoy, A. J., & Plomp, R. (1983). The effect of a hearing aid on the speech-reception threshold of hearing-impaired listeners in quiet and in noise. *Journal of the Acoustical Society of America, 73,* 2166–2173.

Ehri, L. C., & Wilce, L. S. (1980). The influence of orthography on readers' conceptualization of the phonemic structure of words. *Applied Psycholinguistics, 1,* 371–385.

Eimas, P. D., Siqueland, E. R., Jusczyk, P., & Vigorito, J. (1971). Speech perception in infants. *Science, 171,* 303–306.

Elfner, L. F., & Homick, J. L. (1967). Continuity effects with alternately sounding tones under dichotic presentation. *Perception & Psychophysics, 2,* 34–36.

Elliott, L. L. (1979). Performance of children aged 9 to 17 years on a test of speech intelligibility in noise using sentence material with controlled word predictability. *Journal of the Acoustical Society of America, 66,* 651–653.

Ferguson, C. A., & Farwell, C. B. (1975). Words and sounds in early language acquisition. *Language, 51,* 419–439.

Festen, J. M., & Plomp, R. (1990). Effects of fluctuating noise and interfering speech on the speech-reception threshold for impaired and normal hearing. *Journal of the Acoustical Society of America, 88,* 1725–1736.

Fowler, C. A. (1987). Perceivers as realists, talkers too: Commentary on papers by Strange, Diehl et al., and Rakerd and Verbrugge. *Journal of Memory and Language, 26,* 574–587.

Fry, D. B., Abramson, A. S., Eimas, P. D., & Liberman, A. M. (1962). The identification and discrimination of synthetic vowels. *Language and Speech, 5,* 171–189.

Gardner, H. (1985). *The mind's new science—A history of the cognitive revolution.* New York: Basic Books.

Gelb, I. J. (1963). *A study of writing.* Chicago: University of Chicago Press.

Gough, P. B., Juel, C., & Griffith, P. L. (1992). Reading, spelling, and the orthographic cipher. In P. B. Gough, L. C. Ehri, & R. Treiman (Eds.), *Reading acquisition* (pp. 35–48). Hillsdale, NJ: Lawrence Erlbaum Associates.

Grose, J. H., & Hall, J. W. (1989). Comodulation masking release using SAM tonal complex maskers: Effects of modulation depth and signal position. *Journal of the Acoustical Society of America, 85,* 1276–1284.

Grosjean, F. (1985). The recognition of words after their acoustic offset: Evidence and implications. *Perception & Psychophysics, 38,* 299–310.

Hall, J. W., Haggard, M. P., & Fernandes, M. A. (1984). Detection in noise by spectrotemporal pattern analysis. *Journal of the Acoustical Society of America, 76,* 50–56.

Hallé, P. A., & de Boysson-Bardies, B. (1994). Emergence of an early receptive lexicon: Infants' recognition of words. *Infant Behavior and Development, 17,* 119–129.

Handel, S. (1989). *Listening. An introduction to the perception of auditory events.* Cambridge, MA: MIT Press.

Harnad, S. (Ed.). (1987). *Categorical perception: The groundwork of cognition.* Cambridge, UK: Cambridge University Press.

Harris, C. M. (1953). A study of the building blocks in speech. *Journal of the Acoustical Society of America, 25,* 962–969.

Harris, R. (1980). *The language-makers.* London: Duckworth.

Heise, G. A., & Miller, G. A. (1951). An experimental study of auditory patterns. *American Journal of Psychology, 64,* 68–77.

Hockett, C. F. (1955). *A manual of phonology.* Baltimore, MD: Waverley Press.

Holloway, C. M. (1970). Passing the strongly voiced components of noisy speech. *Nature, 226,* 178–179.

Houtgast, T. (1973). Psychophysical experiments on "tuning curves" and "two-tone inhibition." *Acustica, 29,* 168–179.

Houtgast, T. (1976). Subharmonic pitches of a pure tone at low S/N ratio. *Journal of the Acoustical Society of America, 90,* 405–409.

Houtsma, A. J. M., & Goldstein, J. L. (1972). The central origin of the pitch of complex tones: Evidence from musical interval recognition. *Journal of the Acoustical Society of America, 51,* 520–529.

Houtsma, A. J. M., & Smurzynski, J. (1990). Pitch identification and discrimination for complex tones with many harmonics. *Journal of the Acoustical Society of America, 87,* 304–310.

Howes, D. (1957).On the relation between the intelligibility and frequency of occurrence of English words. *Journal of the Acoustical Society of America, 29,* 296–305.

Huey, E. B. (1968). *The psychology and pedagogy of reading.* Cambridge, MA: Massachusetts Institute of Technology Press. (Original work published 1908.)

Huttenlocher, J., & Goodman, J. (1987). The time to identify spoken words. In A. Allport, D. MacKay, W. Prinz, & E. Scheerer (Eds.), *Language perception and production* (pp. 431–444). London: Academic Press.

Ingram, D. (1974). Phonological rules in young children. *Journal of Child Language, 1,* 49–64.

Iverson, P., & Krumhansl, C. L. (1993). Isolating the dynamic attributes of musical timbre. *Journal of the Acoustical Society of America, 94,* 2595–2603.

Jones, D. (1976). *The phoneme: Its nature and use.* Cambridge, UK: Cambridge University Press. (Original work published 1950.)

Joos, M. (1948). Acoustic phonetics. *Language, 24, Language Monographs No. 23.*

Jusczyk, P. (1995). Language acquisition: Speech sounds and the beginning of phonology. In J. L. Miller & P. D. Eimas (Eds.), *Handbook of perception and cognition: Speech, language, and communication* (2nd ed., pp. 263–301). San Diego, CA: Academic Press.

Jusczyk, P., & Aslin, R. N. (1995). Infants' detection of the sound patterns of words in fluent speech. *Cognitive Psychology, 29,* 1–23.

Jusczyk, P. W., Friederici, A. D., Wessels, J. M. I., Svenkerud, V. Y., & Jusczyk, A. M. (1993). Infants' sensitivity to the sound patterns of native language words. *Journal of Memory and Language, 32,* 402–420.

Jusczyk, P., Houston, D., & Goodman, M. (1998). Speech perception during the first year. In A. Slater (Ed.), *Perceptual development: Visual, auditory, and speech perception* (pp. 357–388). Hove, UK: Psychology Press.

Katz, N., Baker, E., & Macnamara, J. (1974). What's in a name? A study of how children learn common and proper names. *Child Development, 45,* 469–473.

Kellman, P. J., & Spelke, E. S. (1983). Perception of partly occluded objects in infancy. *Cognitive Psychology, 15,* 483–524.

Klatt, D. H. (1982). Prediction of perceived phonetic distance from critical-band spectra: A first step. *Proceedings of the International Conference on Acoustics, Speech, and Signal Processing* (pp. 1278–1281). New York: IEEE.

Klatt, D. H. (1989). Review of selected models of speech perception. In W. Marslen-Wilson (Ed.), *Lexical representation and process* (pp. 169–226). Cambridge, MA: MIT Press.

Klein, W., Plomp, R., & Pols, L. C. W. (1970). Vowel spectra, vowel spaces, and vowel identification. *Journal of the Acoustical Society of America, 48,* 999–1009.

Kluender, K. R., Diehl, R. L., & Killeen, P. R. (1987). Japanese quail can learn phonetic categories. *Science, 237,* 1195–1197.

Kolers, P. A. (1972). Experiments in reading. *Scientific American, 227,* 84–91.

Koopmans-van Beinum, F. J. (1980). *Vowel contrast reduction: An acoustic and perceptual study of Dutch vowels in various speech conditions.* Doctoral thesis, University of Amsterdam.

Kruskal, J. B. (1964). Nonmetric multidimensional scaling: A numerical method. *Psychometrika, 29,* 115–129.

Kučera, H., & Francis, W. N. (1967). *Computational analysis of present-day American English.* Providence, RI: Brown University Press.

Kuhl, P. K. (1987a). The special-mechanisms debate in speech research: Categorization tests on animals and infants. In S. Harnad (Ed.), *Categorical perception: The groundwork of cognition* (pp. 355–386). Cambridge, UK: Cambridge University Press.

Kuhl, P. K. (1987b). Perception of speech and sound in early infancy. In P. Salapatek & L. Cohen (Eds.), *Handbook of infant perception* (Vol. 2, pp. 275–382). New York: Academic Press.

Ladefoged, P. (1967). *Three areas of experimental phonetics.* London: Oxford University Press.

Ladefoged, P., & Broadbent, D. E. (1957). Information conveyed by vowels. *Journal of the Acoustical Society of America, 29,* 98–104.

Lane, H. (1965). The motor theory of speech perception: A critical review. *Psychological Review, 72,* 275–309.

Lauter, J. L. (1999). Functional asymmetries and the Trimodal Brain: Dimensions and individual differences. *Journal of Developmental and Learning Disorders, 3,* 181–260.

Lauter, J. L., & Hirsh, I. J. (1985). Speech as temporal pattern: A psychoacoustical profile. *Speech Communication, 4,* 41–54.

Lehr, A. (1959). *De klokkengieters François en Pieter Hemony.* Asten, the Netherlands: Eijsbouts.

Liberman, A. M. (1957). Some results of research on speech perception. *Journal of the Acoustical Society of America, 29,* 117–123.

Liberman, A. M. (1970). The grammars of speech and language. *Cognitive Psychology, 1,* 301–323.

Liberman, A. M. (1996). *Speech: A special code.* Cambridge, MA: MIT Press.

Liberman, A. M., Cooper, F. S., Shankweiler, D. P., & Studdert-Kennedy, M. (1967). Perception of the speech code. *Psychological Review, 74,* 431–461.

Liberman, A. M., Delattre, P., & Cooper, F. S. (1952). The role of selected stimulus-variables in the perception of the unvoiced stop consonants. *American Journal of Psychology, 65,* 497–516.

Liberman, A. M., Harris, K. S., Hoffman, H. S., & Griffith, B. C. (1957). The discrimination of speech sounds within and across phoneme boundaries. *Journal of Experimental Psychology, 54,* 358–368.

Liberman, A. M., & Mattingly, I. G. (1985). The motor theory of speech perception revised. *Cognition, 21,* 1–36.

Liberman, I. Y., Shankweiler, D., Fischer, F. W., & Carter, B. (1974). Explicit syllable and phoneme segmentation in the young child. *Journal of Experimental Child Psychology, 18,* 201–212.

Licklider, J. C. R. (1952). On the process of speech perception. *Journal of the Acoustical Society of America, 24,* 590–594.

Licklider, J. C. R. (1954). "Periodicity" pitch and "place" pitch. *Journal of the Acoustical Society of America, 26,* 945.

Lindamood, P., Bell, N., & Lindamood, P. (1997). Achieving competence in language and literacy by training in phonemic awareness, concept imagery and comparator function. In C. Hulme & M. Snowling (Eds.), *Dyslexia: Biology, cognition and intervention* (pp. 212–234). London: Whur.

Lively, S. E., Pisoni, D. B., & Goldinger, S. D. (1994). Spoken word recognition—Research and theory. In M. A. Gernsbacher (Ed.), *Handbook of psycholinguistics* (pp. 265–301). San Diego, CA: Academic Press.

Loftus, E. F. (1991). The glitter of everyday memory ... and the gold. *American Psychologist, 46,* 16–18.

Luce, P. A. (1986). A computational analysis of uniqueness points in auditory word recognition. *Perception & Psychophysics, 39,* 155–158.

Luce, P. A., & Pisoni, D. B. (1998). Recognizing spoken words: The neighborhood activation model. *Ear & Hearing, 19,* 1–36.

Lüdtke, H. (1969). Die Alphabetschrift und das Problem der Lautsegmentierung. *Phonetica, 20,* 147–176.

Manguel, A. (1996). *A history of reading.* London: Harper Collins.

Marslen-Wilson, W. D., & Welsh, A. (1978). Processing interactions and lexical access during word recognition in continuous speech. *Cognitive Psychology, 10,* 29–63.

Massaro, D. W. (1994). Psychological aspects of speech perception—Implications for research and theory. In M. A. Gernsbacher (Ed.), *Handbook of psycholinguistics* (pp. 219–263). San Diego, CA: Academic Press.

Mattingly, I. G., & Studdert-Kennedy, M. (Eds.). (1991). *Modularity and the motor theory of speech perception.* Hillsdale, NJ: Lawrence Erlbaum Associates.

McClelland, J. L., & Elman, J. L. (1986). The TRACE model of speech perception. *Cognitive Psychology, 18,* 1–86.

Mehler, J., Segui, J, & Frauenfelder, U. (1981). The role of the syllable in language acquisition and perception. In T. Myers, J. Laver, & J. Anderson (Eds.), *The cognitive representation of speech* (pp. 295–311). Amsterdam: North-Holland Publishing Company.

Menn, L. (1978). Phonological units in beginning speech. In A. Bell & J. B. Hooper (Eds.), *Syllables and segments* (pp. 157–171). Amsterdam: North-Holland.

Mersenne, M. (1636). *Traité des instrumens*, Book IV, Prop. 11, (pp. 208–209). Paris: Sebastian Cramoisy. English translation from C. Truesdell, *The rational mechanics of flexible or elastic bodies, 1638–1788*, Leonhardi Euleri Opera Omnia Ser. II, Vol. 11, Part 2, p. 32 (1960). Zürich: Orell Füssli.

Metzger, W. (1953). *Gesetze des Sehens*. Frankfurt am Main, Germany: Waldemar Kramer.

Middelweerd, M. J., & Plomp, R. (1987). The effect of speechreading on the speech-reception threshold of sentences in noise. *Journal of the Acoustical Society of America, 82*, 2145–2147.

Miller, G. A. (1991). *The science of words*. New York, NY: Scientific American Library.

Miller, G. A., & Friedman, E. A. (1957). The reconstruction of mutilated English texts. *Information and Control, 1*, 38–55.

Miller, G. A., & Heise, G. A. (1950). The trill threshold. *Journal of the Acoustical Society of America, 22*, 637–638.

Miller, G. A., Heise, G. A., & Lichten, W. (1951). The intelligibility of speech as a function of the context of the test materials. *Journal of Experimental Psychology, 41*, 329–335.

Miller, G. A., & Isard, S. (1963). Some perceptual consequences of linguistic rules. *Journal of Verbal Learning and Verbal Behavior, 2*, 217–228.

Miller, G. A., & Licklider, J. C. R. (1950). The intelligibility of interrupted speech. *Journal of the Acoustical Society of America, 22*, 167–173.

Miller, J. D. (1989). Auditory-perceptual interpretation of the vowel. *Journal of the Acoustical Society of America, 85*, 2114–2134.

Miller, J. L., & Eimas, P. D. (1995). Speech perception: From signal to word. *Annual Review of Psychology, 46*, 467–492.

Miller, J. L., Grosjean, F., & Lomanto, C. (1984). Articulation rate and its variability in spontaneous speech: A reanalysis and some implications. *Phonetica, 41*, 215–225.

Moore, B. C. J., & Ohgushi, K. (1993). Audibility of partials in inharmonic complex tones. *Journal of the Acoustical Society of America, 93*, 452–461.

Moore, R. K. (1981). Speech recognition systems and theories of speech perception. In T. Myers, J. Laver, & J. Anderson (Eds.), *The cognitive representation of speech* (pp. 427–441). Amsterdam: North-Holland Publishing Company.

Morais, J., Cary, L., Alegria, J., & Bertelson, P. (1979). Does awareness of speech as a sequence of phones arise spontaneously? *Cognition, 7*, 323–331.

Morais, J., & Kolinsky, R. (1995). The consequences of phonemic awareness. In B. de Gelder & J. Morais (Eds.), *Speech and Reading: A comparative approach* (pp. 317–337). Hillsdale, NJ: Lawrence Erlbaum Associates.

Morrow, C. T. (1971). Speech in deep-submergence atmospheres. *Journal of the Acoustical Society of America, 50*, 715–728.

Neisser, U. (1978). Memory: What are the important questions? In M. M. Gruneberg, P. E. Morris, and R. N. Sykes (Eds.), *Practical aspects of memory* (pp. 3–24). London: Academic Press.

Newman, R. S., & Jusczyk, P. W. (1996). The cocktail party effect in infants. *Perception & Psychophysics, 58*, 1145–1156.

Nittrouer, S., & Studdert-Kennedy, M. (1987). The role of coarticulatory effects in the perception of fricatives by children and adults. *Journal of Speech and Hearing Research, 30*, 319–329.

Nooteboom, S. G. (1981). Speech rate and segmental perception or the role of words in phoneme identification. In T. Myers, J. Laver, & J. Anderson (Eds.), *The cognitive representation of speech* (pp. 143–150). Amsterdam: North-Holland.

Nooteboom, S. G., Brokx, J. P. L., & de Rooij, J. J. (1976). Contributions of prosody to speech perception. In W. J. M. Levelt & G. B. Flores d'Arcais (Eds.), *Studies in the perception of language* (pp. 75–107). Chichester, UK: Wiley.

Norris, D. (1994). Shortlist: A connectionist model of continuous speech recognition. *Cognition, 52,* 189–234.

Nygaard, L. C., & Pisoni, D. B. (1995). Speech perception: New directions in research and theory. In J. L. Miller & P. D. Eimas (Eds.), *Handbook of perception and cognition: Speech, language, and communication* (2nd ed., pp. 63–96). San Diego, CA: Academic Press.

Ohm, G. S. (1843). Über die Definition des Tones, nebst daran geknüpfter Theorie der Sirene und ähnlicher tonbildender Vorrichtungen. *Annalen der Physik und Chemie, 59,* 513–565.

Oller, D. K., and Eilers, R. E. (1988). The role of audition in infant babbling. *Child Development, 59,* 441–449.

O'Regan, J. K. (1990). Eye movements and reading. In E. Kowler (Ed.), *Eye movements and their role in visual cognitive processes* (pp. 395–453). Amsterdam: Elsevier.

O'Regan, J. K., Lévy-Schoen, A., & Jacobs, A. M. (1983). The effect of visibility on eye-movement parameters in reading. *Perception & Psychophysics, 34,* 457–464.

Pickett, J. M., & Pollack, I. (1963). Intelligibility of excerpts from fluent speech: Effects of rate of utterance and duration of excerpt. *Language and Speech, 6,* 151–164.

Pisoni, D. B., & Lazarus, J. H. (1974). Categorical and noncategorical modes of speech perception along the voicing continuum. *Journal of the Acoustical Society of America, 55,* 328–333.

Planck, M. (1998). *Eight lectures on theoretical physics, delivered at Columbia University in 1909.* New York: Dover. (Original work published 1915.)

Plomp, R. (1967). Pitch of complex tones. *Journal of the Acoustical Society of America, 41,* 1526–1533.

Plomp, R. (1976). *Aspects of tone sensation—A psychophysical study.* New York: Academic Press.

Plomp, R. (1986). A signal-to-noise ratio model for the speech-reception threshold of the hearing impaired. *Journal of Speech and Hearing Research, 29,* 146–154.

Plomp, R., & Mimpen, A. M. (1964). The ear as a frequency analyzer. *Journal of the Acoustical Society of America, 36,* 1628–1636.

Plomp, R., & Mimpen, A. M. (1968). The ear as a frequency analyzer. II. *Journal of the Acoustical Society of America, 43,* 764–767.

Plomp, R., & Steeneken, H. J. M. (1969). Effect of phase on the timbre of complex tones. *Journal of the Acoustical Society of America, 46,* 409–421.

Plomp, R., & Steeneken, H. J. M. (1973). Place dependence of timbre in reverberant sound fields. *Acustica, 28,* 50–59.

Poffenberger, A. T. (Ed.). (1947). *1860–1944—James McKeen Cattell—Man of science, Vol. 1, Psychological research.* Lancaster, PA: Science Press.

Pollack, I., & Pickett, J. M. (1963). The intelligibility of excerpts from conversation. *Language and Speech, 6,* 165–171.

Pols, L. C. W. (1971). Real-time recognition of spoken words. *IEEE Transactions on Computers, C-20,* 972–978.

Pols, L. C. W., Tromp, H. R. C., & Plomp, R. (1973). Frequency analysis of Dutch vowels from 50 male speakers. *Journal of the Acoustical Society of America, 53,* 1093–1101.

Pols, L. C. W., van der Kamp, L. J. T., & Plomp, R. (1969). Perceptual and physical space of vowel sounds. *Journal of the Acoustical Society of America, 46,* 458–467.

Potter, R. K. (1945). Visible patterns of sound. *Science, 102,* 463–470.

Potter, R. K., Kopp, G. A., & Green, H. C. (1947). *Visible speech.* New York: Van Nostrand.

Powers, G. L., & Wilcox, J. C. (1977). Intelligibility of temporally interrupted speech with and without intervening noise. *Journal of the Acoustical Society of America, 61,* 195–199.

Rayner, K., & Bertera, J. H. (1979). Reading without a fovea. *Science, 206,* 468–469.

Read, C., Yun-fei, Z., Hong-yin, N., & Bao-qing, D. (1986). The ability to manipulate speech sounds depends on knowing alphabetic writing. *Cognition, 24,* 31–44.

Remez, R. E., & Rubin, P. E. (1984). On the perception of intonation from sinusoidal sentences. *Perception & Psychophysics, 35,* 429–440.

Remez, R. E., Rubin, P. E., Pisoni, D. B., & Carrell, T. D. (1981). Speech perception without traditional speech cues. *Science, 212,* 947–950.

Repp, B. H. (1981). On levels of description in speech research. *Journal of the Acoustical Society of America, 69,* 1462–1464.

Ritsma, R. J. (1962). Existence region of the tonal residue. I. *Journal of the Acoustical Society of America, 34,* 1224–1229.

Rosner, B. S., & Pickering, J. B. (1994). *Vowel perception and production.* Oxford, UK: Oxford University Press.

Sakamoto, T., & Makita, K. (1973). Japan. In J. Downing (Ed.), *Comparative reading. Cross-national studies of behavior and processes in reading and writing* (pp. 440–465). New York: Macmillan.

Samuel, A. G. (1977). The effect of discrimination training on speech perception: Noncategorical perception. *Perception & Psychophysics, 22,* 321–330.

Savin, H. B., & Bever, T. G. (1970). The nonperceptual reality of the phoneme. *Journal of Verbal Learning and Verbal Behavior, 9,* 295–302.

Scharf, B. (1964). Partial masking. *Acustica, 14,* 16–23.

Schouten J. F. (1938). The perception of subjective tones. *Proceedings van de Koninklijke Nederlandse Akademie van Wetenschappen, 41,* 1086–1093.

Schouten, J. F. (1940). The residue, a new component in subjective sound analysis. *Proceedings van de Koninklijke Nederlandse Akademie van Wetenschappen, 43,* 356–365.

Schouten, J. F., Ritsma, R. J., & Cardozo, B. L. (1962). Pitch of the residue. *Journal of the Acoustical Society of America, 34,* 1418–1424.

Schouten, M. E. H., & Pols, L. C. W. (1979). CV- and VC-transitions: A spectral study of coarticulation—Part II. *Journal of Phonetics, 7,* 205–224.

Scragg, D. G. (1974). *A history of English spelling.* Manchester, UK: Manchester University Press.

Seebeck, A. (1841). Beobachtungen über einige Bedingungen der Entstehung von Tönen. *Annalen der Physik und Chemie, 53,* 417–436.

Segui, J., Frauenfelder, U., & Mehler, J. (1981). Phoneme monitoring, syllable monitoring and lexical access. *British Journal of Psychology, 72,* 471–477.

Shannon, R. V., Zeng, F. G., Kamath, V., Wygonski, J., & Ekelid, M. (1995). Speech recognition with primarily temporal cues. *Science, 270,* 303–304.

Shockey, L., & Reddy, R. (1975). Quantitative analysis of speech perception: Results from transcription of connected speech from unfamiliar languages. In G. Fant (Ed.), *Proceedings of the Speech Communication Seminar.* Stockholm.

Shriberg, E. (1992). Perceptual restoration of filtered vowels with added noise. *Language and Speech, 35,* 127–136.

Siegel, J. A., & Siegel, W. (1977). Categorical perception of tonal intervals: Musicians can't tell sharp from flat. *Perception & Psychophysics, 21,* 399–407.

Slater, A., Morison, V., Somers, M., Mattock, A., Brown, E., & Taylor, D. (1990). Newborns and older infants' perception of partly occluded objects. *Infant Behavior and Development, 13,* 33–49.

Smoorenburg, G. F. (1970). Pitch perception of two-frequency stimuli. *Journal of the Acoustical Society of America, 48,* 924–942.

Spelke, E. S., Breinlinger, K., Macomber, J., & Jacobson, K. (1992). Origins of knowledge. *Psychological Review, 99,* 605–632.

Spencer, N. J., & Wollman, N. (1980). Lexical access for phonetic ambiguities. *Language and Speech, 23,* 171–198.

Stetson, R. H. (1951). *Motor phonetics—A study of speech movements in action.* Amsterdam: North-Holland.

Stevens, K. N., & Blumstein, S. E. (1978). Invariant cues for place of articulation in stop consonants. *Journal of the Acoustical Society of America, 64,* 1358–1368.

Stevens, S. S., & Davis, H. (1948). *Hearing—Its psychology and physiology* (3rd ed.). New York: John Wiley & Sons. (Original work published 1938.)

Strange, W. (1989). Evolving theories of vowel perception. *Journal of the Acoustical Society of America, 85,* 2081–2087.

Strange, W., & Bohn, O. S. (1998). Dynamic specification of coarticulated German vowels: Perceptual and acoustical studies. *Journal of the Acoustical Society of America, 104,* 488–504.

Strange, W., Verbrugge, R. R., Shankweiler, D. P., & Edman, T. R. (1976). Consonant environment specifies vowel identity. *Journal of the Acoustical Society of America, 60,* 213–224.

Stroop, J. R. (1935). Studies of interference in serial verbal reactions. *Journal of Experimental Psychology, 18,* 643–662.

Studdert-Kennedy, M. (1987). The phoneme as a perceptuomotor structure. In A. Allport, D. MacKay, W. Prinz, & E. Scheerer (Eds.), *Language perception and production* (pp. 67–84). London: Academic Press.

Tartter, V. C. (1989). What's in a whisper? *Journal of the Acoustical Society of America, 86,* 1678–1683.

ter Keurs, M., Festen, J. M., & Plomp, R. (1992). Effect of spectral envelope smearing on speech reception. I. *Journal of the Acoustical Society of America, 91,* 2872–2880.

ter Keurs, M., Festen, J. M., & Plomp, R. (1993). Effect of spectral envelope smearing on speech reception. II. *Journal of the Acoustical Society of America, 93,* 1547–1552.

Thurlow, W. R. (1957). An auditory figure-ground effect. *American Journal of Psychology, 70,* 653–654.

Thurlow, W. R., & Elfner, L. F. (1959). Continuity effects with alternately sounding tones. *Journal of the Acoustical Society of America, 31,* 1337–1339.

Treiman, R., & Baron, J. (1981). Segmental analysis ability: Development and relation to reading ability. In T. G. Waller & G. E. MacKinnon (Eds.), *Reading research: Advances in theory and practice* (Vol. 3, pp. 159–198). New York: Academic Press.

Uttal, W.R. (1988). *On seeing forms.* Hillsdale, NJ: Lawrence Erlbaum Associates.

van Dijkhuizen, J. N., Anema, P. C., and Plomp, R. (1987). The effect of varying the slope of the amplitude-frequency response on the masked speech-reception threshold of sentences. *Journal of the Acoustical Society of America, 81,* 465–469.

van Noorden, L. P. A. S. (1975). *Temporal coherence in the perception of tone sequences.* Doctoral thesis, Technical University, Eindhoven.

van Son, R. J. J. H., & Pols, L. C. W. (1995). The influence of local context on the identification of vowels and consonants. *Proceedings of Eurospeech* (pp. 967–970). Madrid: 4th European Conference on Speech Communication and Technology.

Verschuure, J., & Brocaar, M. P. (1983). Intelligibility of interrupted meaningful and nonsense speech with and without intervening noise. *Perception & Psychophysics, 33,* 232–240.

Verschuure, J., Rodenburg, M., & Maas, A. J. J. (1976). Presentation conditions of the pulsation threshold method. *Acustica, 35,* 47–54.

von Békésy, G. (1960). *Experiments in hearing.* New York: McGraw-Hill.

von Helmholtz, H. L. F. (1954). *On the sensations of tones as the physiological basis for the theory of music* (Trans. A. J. Ellis). New York: Dover. (Original work published 1863.)

Vroomen, J., van Zon, M., & de Gelder, B. (1996). Cues to speech segmentation: Evidence from juncture misperceptions and vowel spotting. *Memory & Cognition, 24*, 744–755.

Walley, A. C., & Carrell, T. D. (1983). Onset spectra and formant transitions in the adult's and child's perception of place of articulation in stop consonants. *Journal of the Acoustical Society of America, 73*, 1011–1022.

Warren, R. M. (1970). Perceptual restoration of missing speech sounds. *Science, 167*, 392–393.

Warren, R. M. (1974). Auditory temporal discrimination by trained listeners. *Cognitive Psychology, 6*, 237–256.

Warren, R. M. (1981). Discussion. In T. Myers, J. Laver, & J. Anderson (Eds.), *The cognitive representation of speech* (pp. 33–37). Amsterdam: North-Holland.

Warren, R. M., & Byrnes, D. L. (1975). Temporal discrimination of recycled tonal sequences: Pattern matching and naming of order by untrained listeners. *Perception & Psychophysics, 18*, 273–280.

Warren, R. M., Hainsworth, K. R., Brubaker, B. S., Bashford, J. A., & Healy, E. W. (1997). Spectral restoration of speech: Intelligibility is increased by inserting noise in spectral gaps. *Perception & Psychophysics, 59*, 275–283.

Warren, R. M., Obusek, C. J., & Ackroff, J. M. (1972). Auditory induction: Perceptual synthesis of absent sounds. *Science, 176*, 1149–1151.

Warren, R. M., & Warren, R. P. (1970). Auditory illusions and confusions. *Scientific American, 223*, 30–36.

Wheeler, D. D. (1970). Processes in word recognition. *Cognitive Psychology, 1*, 59–85.

Zahorian, S. A., & Jagharghi, A. J. (1993). Spectral-shape features versus formants as acoustic correlates for vowels. *Journal of the Acoustical Society of America, 94*, 1966–1982.

Zahorian, S. A., & Rothenberg, M. (1981). Principal-components analysis for low-redundancy encoding of speech spectra. *Journal of the Acoustical Society of America, 69*, 832–845.

Zipf, G. K. (1965). *Human behavior and the principle of least effort.* New York: Hafner. (Original work published 1949.)

Author Index

A

Abramson, A. S., 140
Ackroff, J. M., 35
Alegria, J., 80
Altmann, G. T. M., 109
Anema, P. C., 103
Aristotle, 85
Ash, M. G., 10
Aslin, R. N., 75

B

Baer, T., 102
Bagley, W. C., 105, 106, 134
Baker, E., 75
Bao-qing, D., 80
Bard, E. G., 109
Baron, J., 82
Bashford, J. A., 47, 48
Bates, E., 76
Beauvois, M. W., 43
Beeckman, I., 16
Békésy, G. von, 32
Bell, N., 81
Benedict, H., 75, 76
Bertelson, P., 80
Bertera, J. H., 118
Besner, D., 119
Best, C. T., 73
Bever, T. G., 114
Bladon, R.A.W., 148
Blauert, J., 54
Bloom, L., 74
Blumstein, S. E., 69
Bohn, O. S., 71
Breeuwer, M., 104

B (continued)

Bregman, A. S., 38, 50
Breinlinger, K., 143
Broadbent, D. E., 95, 96
Brocaar, M. P., 48
Brokx, J. P. L., 123
Bronkhorst, A. W., 55, 123
Bruce, D.J., 77
Buckley, O. E., 62
Burns, E. M., 141
Byrne, B., 79
Byrnes, D. L., 51

C

Cardozo, B. L., 27
Carey, S., 75, 76
Carrell, T. D., 69, 103
Carter, B., 65
Cary, L., 80
Cattell, J. M., 105, 115
Chall, J. S., 81
Cherry, C., 48
Ciocca, V., 38
Clark, E. V., 76
Cohen, G., 8
Cole, R. A., 50, 63, 105, 106, 110
Cooper, F. S., 66
Coulmas, F., 82
Cross, 140
Crystal, T. H., 99
Cutler, A., 109, 110, 152
Cutting, J. E., 50, 51

D

Dahl, H., 111
Dannenbring, G. L., 38, 50

Subject Index